Managing the Learning Function

ASTD LEARNING SYSTEM

Module 6

ASTD PRESS

ASTD Press is an internationally renowned source of insightful and practical information on workplace learning and performance topics, including training basics, evaluation and return-on-investment (ROI), instructional systems development (ISD), e-learning, leadership, and career development.

Ordering information: The *ASTD Learning System* and other books published by ASTD Press can be purchased by visiting our website at http://store.astd.org or by calling 800.628.2783 or 703.683.8100.

Library of Congress Control Number: 2006920961

ISBN-10: 1-56286-444-0

ISBN-13: 978-1-56286-444-6

ASTD Press Staff
Director: Anthony Allen
Manager, Acquisitions and Author Relations: Justin Brusino
Editorial Manager: Larry Fox
Sr. Associate Editor: Tora Estep
Associate Editor: Ashley McDonald
Editorial Assistant: Stephanie Castellano
Production Coordinator: Glenn Saltzman
Cover Design: Alizah Epstein

Composition by Stephen McDougal, Mechanicsville, Maryland, www.alphawebtech.net

Contents

Introduction

The *ASTD Competency Study: Mapping the Future* presents the ASTD Competency Model, which defines the workplace learning and performance (WLP) profession and its success factors and forms the basis for certification. In preparing the report, the authors identified eight trends shaping the field:

1. uncertain economic conditions

2. blurred lines between work and life as a result of new organizational structures

3. changes in the way people connect as a result of global communication technology

4. rising diversity in the workplace

5. increasing rates of change, which requires more adaptable workers and nimbler organizations

6. concerns about security and the safety of intellectual property

7. transformation of the ways that people work and live as a result of technology

8. a higher ethical bar.

Enabling organizations to stay flexible and adaptable in this environment is why managing the learning function is such an important area of expertise (AOE). Managing the learning function encompasses many specific technical skills and knowledge, which can be summed up in the *ASTD Competency Study*'s definition: "Providing leadership in developing human capital to execute the organization's strategy; planning, organizing, monitoring, and adjusting activities associated with the administration of workplace learning and performance." Having a strong learning function allows an organization to adapt to new technologies and changing demographic profiles of employees and customers.

To be proficient in these tasks, WLP professionals must be able to combine the specific skills and knowledge defined in key knowledge areas with an appropriate use of foundational competencies. Foundational competencies are grouped into three clusters in the model: interpersonal, business/management, and personal. In essence, these are skills that are relevant to all learning and performance professionals, no matter what their job titles.

More specific to the AOE, WLP professionals need to know about the key knowledge areas that are defined in the *ASTD Competency Study*, which, when expanded, form the chapters of the *ASTD Learning System*. They comprise background information, procedures, tools, issues, best practices, and so forth that are necessary to be expert in an AOE. For managing the learning function, key knowledge areas include learning technologies; ***learning information systems***; marketplace resources; understanding program administration; budgeting, accounting, and financial management; principles of management; project-management tools and processes; human resources systems; business model, drivers, and competitive position; external systems; and legal, regulatory, and ethical requirements.

WLP professionals also need to understand key knowledge related to other areas of expertise. These appear as crossovers in the *ASTD Learning System*. For *Managing the Learning Function*, crossover chapters cover needs assessment methods and identification, adult learning theories, and learning design theory, which are all described in greater detail in Module 1: *Designing Learning*, and communication and influence, which is explained in greater detail in Module 5: *Facilitating Organizational Change*.

Closely related to key knowledge are key actions. Key actions are the behaviors and activities required for a WLP professional to perform effectively in an AOE. If key knowledge is what learning professionals know, then key actions are what they do. In managing the learning function, one important key action is establishing a ***vision***, which involves creating a compelling image of how the learning function can improve the performance of the business and enable execution of the organization's strategy. To do this, the WLP professional needs to understand the organization's business model, drivers, and competitive position in the industry. Other important key actions are establishing strategies and implementing action plans, which require knowledge of ***project management***, learning technologies and learning information systems, marketplace resources, and more.

Key actions lead to outcomes. Outcomes are what the WLP professional delivers. The table on the next page lists the key actions described for the AOE in the *ASTD Competency Study* along with some examples of outputs that arise from these actions.

Key Actions (Do)	Examples of Outcomes (Deliver)
• Establish a vision • Establish strategies	• Learning and development proposals • Human resource strategy white papers
• Implement action plans • Develop and monitor the budget • Manage staff • Model leadership in developing people • Ensure compliance with legal, ethical, and regulatory requirements	• Fulfilled learning plans • Improved human and organizational performance • Status reports for managers (on development of their staff members)
• Manage external resources	• Requests for proposals

For further detailed information about the key actions and outputs, refer to the *ASTD Competency Study: Mapping the Future* (2004).*

*Bernthal, P.R., et al. (2004). *The ASTD Competency Study: Mapping the Future.* Alexandria, VA: ASTD Press.

1
Needs Assessment Methods and Identification

 Needs assessments in training is a systematic, preliminary process of identifying how training can help an organization reach its goals. It is the process of collecting and synthesizing data. Without needs assessment, trainers risk developing and delivering training that does not support organizational needs and, therefore, does not deliver value to the organization and may not be accepted by participants.

These are the main purposes of conducting a **_training needs assessment_**:

- It places the training need or request in the context of the organization's needs. Training adds value only when it ultimately serves a business need.

- It validates and augments the initial issues presented by the client.

- It ensures that the ultimate training design supports employee performance and thereby helps the organization meet its needs.

- It results in recommendations regarding nontraining issues that affect the achievement of desired organizational and employee performance goals.

- It helps ensure survival of the training function.

- It establishes the foundation for back-end **_evaluation_**.

These are the seven steps involved in conducting a training needs assessment:

1. External and internal organizational scan

2. Data collection to identify business needs

3. Identification of potential training solutions

4. Data collection to identify performance, learning, and learner needs

5. Data analysis

6. Delivery of data analysis feedback

7. Transition step that begins the training design process.

Learning Objective:

☑ Explain the importance and purpose of conducting a human performance improvement needs assessment.

Key Knowledge: A Human Performance Improvement Needs Assessment Perspective

Why should workplace learning and performance (WLP) professionals emphasize needs assessment and analysis? First, they are integral to WLP. Second, WLP professionals are expected to ensure that an organization's employees can perform the work required for business success. Needs assessment and analysis are the means of measuring a results gap and demonstrating whether a WLP initiative has closed the identified gap.

From a human performance improvement perspective, training design should begin only after a fundamental front-end problem analysis yields a go (as opposed to a no go) signal. Joe Harless (2000), author of *Analyzing Human Performance: Tools for Achieving Business Results*, points out that when trainers, managers, supervisors, or employees perceive a performance problem, training may be the solution, part of the solution, or unrelated to the solution. For this reason, WLP professionals should ask these questions:

- What indicators or symptoms suggest that change is needed?
- What is the root of the problem?
- What role, if any, can training play in remedying the problem?
- What is the monetary value of solving the problem?
- Would an improvement—but less than complete remedy—be acceptable?

If the WLP professional finds that training is needed, the analysis phase of ***instructional systems development*** continues, and ***instructional designers*** might start sketching out a design while considering resources and constraints of time, money, culture, training population characteristics, availability, and location.

Data gathering is a widely used skill in a designer's tool kit. Whether used for front-end assessment of needs and context or back-end evaluation of the effect of training, a designer's skill set must include designing and using a variety of assessment methodologies. For data-gathering tools to be effective, a designer must understand key principles for a range of techniques and know how to collate, synthesize, and interpret the resulting information in an open-minded way.

For more information, see Module 1, *Designing Learning,* chapter 7, "Assessment Methods and Formats."

2
Adult Learning Theories

 Adult learning theories are the foundation for developing and delivering training for the adult learner. **Training managers** require a thorough understanding of adult learning theories to guide the design and delivery of training programs. Knowing how adults learn helps ensure that the instructional design meets learners' needs.

The body of knowledge for adult learning supports three specific training areas: design of programs and materials, delivery methods, and participant needs based on learning characteristics. Many theories, models, and concepts of adult learning overlap across those three areas and focus on them individually.

The first training area involves the role of adult learning theories in designing materials to reach each learner, which supports program design and delivery methods. It's important to recognize that every learner is unique, but designing learning programs that engage all learners is possible. The four theories of learning and instruction (subject centered, **objective** centered, experience centered, and opportunity centered) determine the focus of program design. For example, a subject-centered program, which is training based on a specific topic, would focus on a subject, such as travel or expense policies. The theories of learning and memory (behaviorism and cognitivism) explain how people learn and retain knowledge with an emphasis on blended learning characteristics across learners. Therefore, design and delivery should not be based on any one theory but integrate all of them.

The second training area addresses delivering training to meet learners' needs, expectations, and individual characteristics. Program and materials design and the instructional format must consider environmental factors that affect learners: stress, job status, peers, supervisors, and the learning and work environments. The delivery format should offer a stimulating and positive learning environment that accommodates adult **learning styles**.

The third training area focuses on how adults learn, which is outlined by the philosophy of **andragogy**, models of learning, and theorists such as Malcolm Knowles and Howard Gardner. This area encompasses adult learners' sense of motivation for learning, sense of self-direction, previous experiences, and need to learn. Satisfying this area acknowledges the needs and goals of learners in the curriculum design and delivery of training and allows them to identify with the need to learn the information based on its relevance to their work.

Learning Objectives:

- ☑ Explain how adult learning theory is incorporated into learning and training.
- ☑ Explain why an understanding of adult learning theory is important for developing and delivering training.

Key Knowledge: Adult Learning Theories

There are many theories on how the mind works and how adults learn best. Having a general understanding of these various theories enables workplace learning and performance (WLP) professionals to apply these theories to the many types of learners as well as to designing and delivering training.

Several important assumptions about adult learners are worth emphasizing. These assumptions help to guide many aspects of adult learning and are often organized by the following categories: adults as learners, motivating adult learners, planning instruction for adults, working with groups of adults, working with individual learners, helping learners transfer what they have learned, and considering the barriers faced by adults in learning.

Most learning professionals will tune out when they hear the word *theory* because they think theory is not practical. However, Kurt Lewin, a founder of modern organizational development, is often credited for saying that "nothing is so practical as a good theory." Theory can guide practice.

How trainers conduct training and how learning professionals carry out other learning and performance change efforts stem from their own theories and philosophies of the learning process, the learners, the learning environment, and the results desired. Almost everything we do is guided by theory.

For WLP professionals, understanding adult learning theories and techniques helps to provide a well-rounded background and a basis for creating and delivering sound instruction. Ultimately these professionals should have an understanding of what theories exist, what they mean, and how they affect practice when delivering training.

Adult learning theories attempt to explain various schools of thought regarding how adults learn. Some theorists focus on observable elements—that is, stimulus and response. Other theorists focus on learning and memory and propose environmental factors and optimal teaching sequences to optimize learning, retention, and long-term memory.

No theory has "right" or "wrong" approaches. Each theory has its advantages and disadvantages, which implies different roles for learners and may be more appropriate than others depending on the mode of delivery, the types of knowledge or skills to be trained, how often the skills will be used, if rote memorization/reaction is required, and so on.

For more information, see Module 1, *Designing Learning,* chapter 1, "Cognition and Adult Learning Theory."

3
Learning Design Theory

 The manager of a learning function needs a broad understanding of what learning or training can accomplish and what organizational issues training can't address. Knowing exactly what clients need help improving (such as business goals) is the first step in determining whether the learning function can provide a training solution. From business goals come learning objectives. Workplace learning and performance (WLP) professionals must pay close attention to an organization's constraints, target population, objectives, and political implications when analyzing needs and deciding between options, such as internal and external courses, forms of open learning, and on-the-job and off-the-job training. Communicating to client groups what the training department can or can't offer is essential, and WLP professionals must be able to educate clients on the limitations of training.

Training objectives must be unambiguous statements that describe precisely what trainees are expected to be able to do as a result of their learning experience. Creating a suitable environment to ensure that training objectives can be achieved is also important.

Although there are many learning theories and schools of thought, WLP professionals should use a systematic process, many of which are based on the classic instructional systems development (ISD) model known as the *ADDIE* model (analysis, design, development, implementation, and evaluation) when designing instruction. No matter which ISD model is used, they all emphasize the need for goals and objectives for instruction and related assessments.

From an instructional designer's perspective, any undertaking that includes a learner and a subject matter to learn requires an *instructional system*. According to Chuck Hodell, author of *ISD From the Ground Up* (2000), to build a training course, instructional designers need inputs, such as subject matter and resources; an ISD process; and outputs, such as curriculum and materials. This combination of elements is called an instructional system.

Learning Objectives:

☑ Describe why it is critical to understand what training can and cannot accomplish.

☑ State the first steps to approaching a learning initiative.

Key Knowledge: ISD Theory and Methods

After a performance gap is identified, a training initiative may be the appropriate solution if the cause of the performance gap is lack of knowledge or skill. ISD is based on the belief that training is most effective when it provides learners with a clear statement of what they must be able to do as a result of training and how their performance will be evaluated.

A number of ISD models, for example Seels and Glasgow or Smith and Ragan, are named after individuals or institutions, but almost all models are based on the ADDIE model, which has five elements:

Analysis: Analysis involves the who, what, where, when, why, and by whom of the design process. Just as *A* is the first letter in the alphabet, analysis should be the first item addressed in instructional design. Analysis is done for one reason: to find out what learners need to know to be successful.

Design: In this phase, the instructional designer provides the basic foundation, structure, and sequence for the training project, including goals, objectives, and evaluation tasks. The structure comes from the many decisions that must be made on training platforms and other implementation questions.

Development: Development is the phase in which instructional designers convert design plans into course materials. For example, for classroom courses, designers may develop slides, lecture notes, and handouts for the course. They may also develop the instructor's materials for administering learning activities and other support materials.

Implementation: Implementation involves more than distributing workbooks and teaching classes. Implementation also involves ongoing support—for example, scheduling class or **web-based training** sessions, instructors, classrooms, and audiovisual and lab equipment; reproducing materials; and updating content on **intranets** and for self-paced learning courses.

Evaluation: Although evaluation appears to be the last function, in reality, it takes place at every point in the ISD process. Evaluation is the ultimate phase in the process of designing a training course. It assesses whether the course achieved its objectives. Evaluation occurs on a number of levels, following a model first proposed in 1959 by Donald Kirkpatrick (1998). The four levels of evaluation are reaction, learning, behavior, and results.

For more information, see Module 1, *Designing Learning,* chapter 2, "Instructional Design Theory and Process."

4
Learning Technologies

Technology is changing the way learning occurs within organizations on a daily basis. Understanding the different technologies available to you and their uses within an organization is critical to providing value-driven training and learning. Management of a learning function requires the development of a diverse network to understand availability, use, and functionality of these technologies. Because technologies can either be a hindrance or an enhancement to learning, the workplace learning and performance (WLP) professional should understand what the technology can do and its advantages and disadvantages.

Learning Objectives:

☑ Describe how learning technologies will support the organization's goals and business objectives.

☑ Identify and select appropriate learning technologies to achieve the desired learning outcomes.

☑ Design instruction by applying appropriate technology-based solutions that support the desired learning outcomes.

☑ Articulate a strategy that seamlessly integrates desired training content with optimal instructional methods, available presentation methods, and the best distribution methods.

☑ Employ evaluation strategies to compare the benefits of one delivery system versus another to choose the most effective model or technology.

☑ Articulate the role that *learning management systems* and knowledge management systems play in developing and employing specific training initiatives for an organization.

☑ Discuss the advantages and disadvantages of various technology-based training solutions, including *computer-based training*, *electronic performance support systems (EPSSs)*, *simulations*, and intranets.

Organizational Strategy as It Relates to Technology

Technology has had an immeasurable effect on the way we learn today, whether the learning takes place formally through structured courses or informally by searching the Internet or collaborating with peers. Learning technology can provide continuous access to training materials, compress learning times by 50 to 60 percent compared to traditional classroom instruction, provide personalized instruction at the learner's own pace, and deliver instruction with optimal consistency.

Most organizations today are in the midst of rapidly changing global competitive markets and are still determined to be world-class companies in the eyes of their stakeholders—customers, owners, employees, and communities. They know this happens only if they deliver the best products, services, performance, results, and innovations in their industry on a sustainable basis.

Strategy drives the direction of an organization and determines the goals and focus for that company. Strategy is defined as identifying the mission and vision of the organization, creating tactical goals and objectives, and translating the goals into action. For WLP professionals, the organizational business strategy should also drive their initiatives and focus when managing the learning function.

In particular, WLP professionals need to develop a strategy for the learning function that is aligned with the CEO's strategic goals. The strategy needs to address not only the learning delivery formats that will be used to address employee development, but also the technologies and investment needed for the learning function to support the business strategy, goals, and objectives.

Organizational Culture

Investment and deployment of technology isn't the only consideration for success of the learning function. The organizational culture plays an enormous role in the success of the learning function when deploying technology-based learning. Think about what happens when a great learning program runs into the barrier of an unsupportive learning culture. The culture always wins.

If learning technologies (including *e-learning*) aren't supported over the long haul by an organization, it will be difficult to keep these efforts going. Marketing helps, but learning technologies can only be sustained when sponsors and learners believe that it is truly beneficial and preferable to traditional instructional approaches so much so that they become advocates themselves.

True learning organizations aren't those with the most courses; they are characterized by the broader culture of open knowledge exchange. For example, do people willingly share what they know? Do they take the time to coach and explain? Do organizational performance management systems encourage knowledge sharing or knowledge hoarding? For technology-based learning solutions to thrive within an organization, the company must have a supportive culture that fosters information flow across organizational and geographic boundaries.

Past Experience With Technology

From the 1970s through the 1990s, companies built bricks-and-mortar training centers at an exponential pace. E-learning courses were available to learners on CD-ROM and were slow and expensive to develop.

The Internet leveled the playing field. Technical roadblocks could now be hurdled, and online training skyrocketed. Everything was moving to technology, and by the early 21st century, corporate training centers were seen as yesterday's news. Web-based courses were cropping up everywhere. Shareable Content Object Reference Model (SCORM) made interoperability more reality than dream, and blended learning soon became the latest watchword—everyone was sprinkling a little classroom instruction and e-learning into programs.

For many WLP professionals today, the biggest struggle is getting learners from different generations to embrace learning content delivered via many new technologies as part of a structured program—and encouraging self-directed learning by accessing content anytime and anywhere to help them perform better on the job.

As a result of the Internet and all of the new technologies that quickly became available to WLP professionals to develop and deliver content to learners, many organizations are reassessing their learning technology investments and questioning the value they are getting for their dollars. Organizations and WLP professionals continue to struggle in defining the success criteria for these solutions.

Support Systems and Overall Goals and Objectives

When implementing any technology solution as part of a learning program, any solution should link to at least one of the organization's goals. When WLP professionals can demonstrate a strategic link to business drivers, it is typically easier to get approval from the executive team.

Most organizations have a technology leadership function that, in conjunction with the CEO and senior leadership team, establishes a technology roadmap for the next 12 months. This roadmap is crucial because it is the recommended information technology (IT) production schedule for the length of the year. If the learning function's requested technology projects are not on the schedule for that year, they might not get supported or funded. WLP professionals need to work with their IT departments to identify project requirements.

Typically learning technology infrastructure will have costs associated with it. Those costs are most likely budgeted by the organization's chief information officer or chief technology officer. WLP professionals will need to research what technology-enabled learning solutions are needed for the upcoming years and how they will be funded. For example, if the organization is rolling out a new sales force automation tool, which the learning function will need to support, how much of the cost to deliver this training will be included in the sales budget versus the learning function budget? It is a good idea to understand how IT budgets are established and note any requirements needed to make a request for IT-related investment in future budgeting cycles.

To help drive technology solutions for the learning function, WLP professionals should get to know the IT team because they can help when maneuvering through the IT application landscape. Taking proactive steps to meet and greet this critical group will help build a positive relationship and build an understanding of the current IT department processes. Researching the technology landscape is mission critical for the learning function to successfully implement technology-enabled solutions.

Technology Selection Process

Technology has changed learning by moving it out of only the classroom and into the workplace, according to Allison Rossett, professor of education technology at San Diego State University. Many studies show that the classroom is less central to training and development today and is growing less central every year. In many cases, the classroom has moved online. Learning enabled by technology now allows learners to gather more data from more sources in targeted and smaller chunks.

Blended learning is now also possible via the advent of technology, which involves a combination of approaches to reach a goal: teaching individually or in a group, in a classroom or while employees are at work, with an instructor, or via technology. Rossett points out that learning is growing more employee-centric, which is both glorious and dangerous. It is glorious because of its closeness to work its targeted nature and because it's multimodal. The danger occurs when employees do not look up information in a knowledge base, don't bother with e-learning modules, and don't take advantage of an e-coach.

WLP professionals determine which technologies are most appropriate for achieving the desired learning outcomes of a program by focusing on the steps discussed below.

Step 1. Identify learning objectives and desired outcomes

The first step in the process of selecting the right technologies for a learning program is the first step in any instructional design process: identifying the learning objectives and tasks and clarifying the desired outcomes the learners must be able to complete for the program to be a success. This step helps to ensure that performance—not technology—is the key driver when creating a learning program.

Step 2. Identify needs of audience and geographical location(s)

As with any analysis phase in the instructional design process, the next step includes understanding the target audience, their demographics, and how geographically dispersed they are.

For example, a learning function needs to provide a learning program for a new sales force automation tool. Most of the sales force is already familiar with the current business processes, which will not change. The new information that they need to know includes how to navigate and enter data in the new system. The sales force is currently located in three countries around the world.

Many constraints will affect which technologies are used, such as the time to create and deploy the solution, budget, geographical time zones, and amount of time that management will allow the sales representatives to be out of the field to attend training.

In this example, the WLP professional responsible for the project decides that everyone must first understand the current business processes before focusing on training the new tool. Perhaps the learning solutions should include a self-paced module on information known as a "refresher" to ensure that everyone has the same baseline knowledge before tackling the new application functionality. If the application functionality is extremely hands-on, then perhaps an instructor-led module either in the classroom or online is appropriate to communicate and build the knowledge and skills on the new tool.

Some specific considerations at this point in the process include listing the available technologies at all locations, assessing the computer skills of the learners, and gathering information regarding any cultural or language considerations.

An example of the type of information that should be gathered and documented during an audience analysis appears in table 4-1.

Table 4-1. Sample Audience Analysis Profile Form

Area	Questions	Findings
BACKGROUND	Range of school experience	
	Native language	
	Cultural considerations	
	Average reading level	
WORK EXPERIENCE	Existing skills or knowledge related to proposed training	
	Variation of work experience levels	
TRAINING	Motivation	
	Recent training experience	
	Effect on current job	
	Degree of accountability	
DELIVERY	Number of people to be trained	
	Location of people to be trained	

Source: Adapted from McArdle (1999).

Step 3. Determine which activities and interactivity are needed

Many WLP professionals struggle with how to get participants interested and involved in learning. Research shows that learners understand concepts better and retain information longer when they are actively involved in the learning process. Therefore, the most effective means of delivering training—no matter what mode of delivery or technology is used—is active training techniques. The key from a technology perspective is that all of the media selected have a definite purpose and have not been selected just for the sake of including technology as part of the solution.

The choice of an appropriate instructional strategy for a particular audience is, at best, a guess if a formal audience analysis has not been conducted as noted in the previous step. One way to match an instructional strategy with a particular audience is to be sensitive to an audience's demographics and preferences. The technology should be suitable for the audience, the content, the organizational environment, and, most of all, the proposed learning objective. These preferences provide WLP professionals with a design template to assist in developing the content and a checklist for making decisions about learning activities.

WLP professionals need to conduct a job analysis (as depicted in table 4-2) to identify the specific tasks that learners need to be able to perform to complete specific job functions. Once the specific tasks are defined, then one can determine the most appropriate instructional strategies, activities, and interactivity for learners to master these tasks.

Some examples of the most common instructional strategies used as part of a learning program include

- lecture
- role play
- group discussion
- self-discovery

Table 4-2. Sample Job Analysis Form

Functional Responsibilities	Tasks Involved
Write 30-minute training module	Define objectives
	Develop topical outline
	Decide on instructional strategies
	Produce course works
Evaluate 30-minute training	Determine level of education
	Include test items in design
	Determine methods of data collection, analysis, and reporting

Source: Adapted from McArdle (1999).

- self-paced or self-programmed instruction
- case studies
- competitive games
- cooperative games
- movies or videos
- individual or group projects
- simulations.

Step 4. Review design considerations

A great number of considerations go into selecting the appropriate technology as part of the solution to engage learners including the type of learning (verbal information, cognitive, or motor skills), audience, demographics, learning styles, number of learners, budget, physical site and resources available, and the facilitators' skills and training style.

Some specific questions that WLP professionals need to confirm at this point are as follows:

- How much interaction is needed among the instructor and the learners?
- Will learners need to work on their own?
- How much support will learners need?
- What resources are needed by the learners?

After these key questions have been answered, the WLP professional needs to consider the advantages and inherent attributes of each technology to determine which one(s) is (are) most appropriate to support the goals and objectives of the learning program. The key is to focus on performance by aligning the learning needs of the target audience with technological capabilities.

Step 5. Construct a rationale for the technology choices

Just as WLP professionals need to develop a rationale for the type of training solution proposed (Is training the right solution to address the problem? If so, then how will the proposed training affect the target audience? What is the acceptance level expected from the audience, supervisors, and management? What is the learning solution effect on the entire organization?), they also need to include a rationale for the types of technologies proposed as part of the learning solution and make a business case for any investment needed by the organization to support this solution. This rationale should address

- benefits to learners
- alignment with organizational strategy and goals
- cost effectiveness.

This rationale should also be supported with a benchmarking analysis and reports to show the current knowledge, skills, and performance metrics for the target audience to help build the business case. These measures and metrics will be critical after training deployment to show the effectiveness of the learning program and the technologies used.

Technical Requirements

After considering the organizational culture, the first hurdle in planning and implementing a training initiative, WLP professionals need to consider the technical requirements. Technology-based learning has set high standards and often requires a high-performance, scalable, and reliable platform to meet baseline user requirements. Users (learners, managers, and administrators) have come to expect a quality experience with any technology-enabled learning solution and generally will reject slow or unreliable solutions. These requirements are the same whether the learning solution is managed behind the firewall on a customer's intranet or through an application service provider. These are some technical requirements when designing, developing, and implementing technology-based solutions within an organization:

- One of the biggest hurdles to overcome is learner resistance and changing the organizational culture's perspective on learning technologies. You don't want to take two steps backward for any gains that you've made with the acceptance and adoption of learning technologies in an organization. Use technology that has proven to be suitable to the task.

- Once learners are able to navigate and access information when they need it to perform on the job, nothing will squash all of these learning design efforts faster than links that do not work or do not direct learners to relevant content. Provide consistent links to related subjects for learning content, and ensure that these links are maintained.

- Tailor the technology requirements as close as possible to the learning environment of the company.

- To facilitate knowledge sharing in an organization, provide an open environment on the Internet for collaboration and discussion. If employees don't have the option to collaborate with each other beyond face-to-face meetings, organizations are missing a significant opportunity to provide access to and leverage experts, break down communications across organizational boundaries, and change the corporate culture.

- The best way to find out what's working well and what needs improvement from a learning technology perspective is to ask for feedback from the learners. Because learning technologies come at an expense, all hard and soft data that can be collected about the effectiveness of technology-based learning solutions is invaluable. Consider using electronic surveys to gather data to help justify the investment in learning technologies and for continuous improvement of learning solutions.

- Learners will only use technologies that they find to be valuable. If the technology is too slow, too difficult to access and navigate, and doesn't provide search capabilities to quickly point learners to what they need, they will soon abandon using the technology. Implement easy-to-use websites, tailored to what the learners want, not what the organization thinks they want.

- Information flows within organizations are often chaotic. Knowledge seekers are trying to get answers to questions, get information or advice to help them with job performance, or seek expert feedback on new ideas. To facilitate the ability to find the right information exactly when it's needed in the organization, consider identifying the work flow of all company processes and information highways including automating forms and processes.

Design/Blend/Develop

Distance learning was one of the first terms used in the early 19th century to describe the distribution of education in a nontraditional manner. Although technology innovators, like Edison, have always been certain that their latest contributions to the media field would be the way to get education to everyone, everywhere, and anytime, technology alone wasn't the answer. Educators soon realized that using a medium for instructional purposes required special instructional design considerations that were different from mainstream application of the medium.

In early technology-based solutions, technology wasn't the only problem. A lack of systematic instructional design was a huge culprit in early failures. It seems strange that organizations were willing to discard their understanding of what makes a good learning solution simply because the delivery method changed. Two factors seemed to drive this:

1. There was a misguided perception that the use of technology eliminated the need for a designer, much in the same way a dishwashing machine eliminated the need to wash dishes by hand.

2. Organizations had already invested so much time and money in purchasing and installing learning technologies that it seemed the best use of resources was to get as much content out to the users as quickly as possible.

A common result was training that did not meet the mark and fell short of the quality standards expected in the traditional setting. Many made the assumption that technology was not the appropriate delivery medium for the content. Although that may have indeed been the case, most of the issues were due to the lack of solid instructional design and assessment techniques.

Before WLP professionals can design effective technology-based solutions, they should have a working knowledge of the newest generation of delivery tools. In particular, WLP professionals should be up to speed on asynchronous e-learning and synchronous virtual learning.

Asynchronous E-Learning

According to the glossary at *Learning Circuits* (Biech 2008), **asynchronous learning** is "learning in which interaction between instructors and students occurs intermittently with a time delay. Examples are self-paced courses taken via the Internet or CD-ROM, Q&A mentoring, online discussion groups, and email."

Asynchronous e-learning became commonplace in the 1980s when content became easily accessible via diskette, CD-ROM, or internal networks. It was adopted by organizations rather quickly because the content could be quickly disseminated to large audiences, who could then participate at a time of their choosing. Although there were early roadblocks that kept asynchronous e-learning from meeting expectations (e.g., much of the content was heavy-text "page-turners" with little interactivity), today this category includes many learning solutions from collaborative discussion boards to self-contained tutorials on the web.

Synchronous Virtual Learning

For WLP professionals who have been working in the field for the last decade or so, the terms *virtual classroom, synchronous learning, live online learning, e-meetings,* and *webinars* all mean basically the same thing—content delivered live over the Internet to geographically dispersed participants.

This category of technologies has great potential for delivering learning solutions to audiences who may otherwise not have the opportunity to participate in a learning event. The implications are tremendous for improving communications among organizations, bridging cultural divides, and providing educational opportunities to global destinations that might be too expensive or time consuming to travel to in person.

When participants encounter programs that do not interest them, when session leaders don't prepare, or when technical goofs slow a program, participants may get the impression that virtual learning is not as effective as traditional classroom training.

Because these technologies are somewhat new, professionals have often been creating programs without the benefit of success models, without best practices, and without full knowledge of how to use the technology to its best advantage. Too often synchronous virtual learning provides participants little or no opportunity for interaction with the course content and too few chances to collaborate with other participants.

Today, virtual learning means you can pull workers off the job for two hours, train them, and get them back to work with a limited interruption to productivity.

Blended Learning

WLP professionals struggle with knowing which media to mix when creating a blended learning solution. A blend is an instructional strategy for delivering on promises of learning and performance. Blending involves a planned combination of approaches, such as coaching by a supervisor, participation in an online class, breakfast with colleagues, competency descriptions, reading, reference to a manual, and participation in workshops or online communities.

A study by Peter Dean and his colleagues found that providing several linked options for learners, in addition to classroom training, increased what they learned. In 2002, Harvard Business School faculty DeLacey and Leonard reported that students learned more when online sessions were added to traditional courses. Student interaction and satisfaction improved as well.

Designing Technology-Based Solutions

When designing technology-based solutions, the same instructional design principles apply, along with some additional considerations. For example, WLP professionals need to align the instructional strategies and content to learning technologies if there is latitude to do so.

Many times WLP professionals do not have a choice in what technologies are used when designing and developing a learning program. They are constrained to use the existing, mandatory technology choices that the organization has already invested in.

When considering technology-based solutions, organizations need to be sure that they are designing learning to address SCORM and 508 compliance requirements. SCORM is the industry standard generated by the U.S. Department of Defense's Advanced Distributed Learning organization that fosters creation of reusable learning content as "instructional objects" within a common technical framework for computer- and web-based learning. SCORM describes that technical framework by providing a harmonized set of guidelines, specifications, and standards.

Another standard, Section 508 of the Americans With Disabilities Act, requires that when federal agencies develop, procure, maintain, or use electronic and information technology (EIT), federal employees with disabilities must have comparable access to and use of information and data as federal employees who have no disabilities, unless an undue burden would be imposed on the agency.

Section 508 also requires that individuals with disabilities who are members of the public seeking information or services from a federal agency have comparable access to and use of information and data as the public without disabilities, unless an undue burden would be imposed on the agency.

Although federal agencies have an explicit statutory obligation to make all EITs that they develop, maintain, or use compliant with Section 508, the current emphasis is on newly procured EITs because it is the category that is explicitly enforceable by legal action.

Options for blended learning go beyond the classroom. Blended learning provides WLP professionals with the opportunity to design learning programs that leverage technology- and nontechnology-based solutions. They are formal and informal, technology- and people-based, independent and convivial, and directive- and discovery-oriented. Essentially blended learning is about developing and using a mix of technologies—such as synchronous web conferences, classroom instruction, and threaded discussions after training.

Table 4-3 lists some categories of technologies for developing training and creating blended learning solutions.

Let's apply these various examples of technologies to an urgent situation with little time for development. For example, you work for a pharmaceutical company and one of your products has received some bad press, which is at many times inaccurate. Every newspaper in the country has raised fears about hormone replacement therapy. The organization now needs to get the right information about the product out quickly to physicians. Patients are concerned and want to switch or stop using the medication and physicians are not sure what information is accurate and how to communicate the technical data correctly to patients.

Notice figure 4-1, which depicts a breakdown of the types of content that could be used in a blended solution and lists which media provides short or longer development timeframes. Due to the circumstances in this particular situation, the content is somewhat stable and the WLP professionals have a short timeframe to create the content and disseminate it. For those reasons, we should focus on the technology solutions that are listed in the left quadrants of the table.

Table 4-3. Categories and Examples of Technologies

Live Face-to-Face (formal) • Instructor-led classrooms • Workshops • Coaching/mentoring • On-the-job training	Live Face-to-Face (informal) • Collegial connections • Work teams • Role modeling
Virtual Collaboration / Synchronous • Live e-learning classes • E-mentoring	Virtual Collaboration / Asynchronous • Email • Online bulletin boards • Listservs • Online communities
Self-Paced Learning • Web learning modules • Online resource links • Simulations • Scenarios • Video and audio CDs/DVDs • Online self-assessments • Workbooks	Performance Support • Help systems • Print job aids • Knowledge databases • Documentation • Performance/decision support tools

Source: Rossett et al. (2003).

Figure 4-1. Learning Option Comparison by Stability and Time to Implement

Workbooks Documentation Online help systems (independent) Live e-learning (archived) Print job aids Collegial connections Role modeling Work teams	Workbooks Documentation Online help systems (integrated) Instructor-led classroom Simulations Scenarios Workshops Web learning modules Video and audio CDs or DVDs Performance/decision support systems	**Stable** ↑ ↓
Work teams Online resource links On-the-job training Online self-assessments Listservs Online bulletin boards Live e-learning (events) Print job aids Email Coaching Online knowledge base	Online communities Live e-learning (classes) Mentoring E-mentoring	**Volatile**

Short Development ←——————→ **Long Development**

Source: Rossett et al. (2003).

For example, some solutions that would meet the short development criteria include

- an online knowledge base to serve as a central repository of information and a directory containing relatively stable content, which is not expected to change often

- coaching over the phone that would allow physicians to process emergent concerns with experts

- a print job aid, produced by experts on the topic that summarizes the benefits and risks of each treatment, combined with a reading list and links to online articles

- a devoted listserv that pushes the very latest information to physicians on a daily or weekly basis

- live online briefings that provide physicians with updates about the latest findings, as well as allowing them to participate in discussions; events with stable content could be archived for later reference, providing value to new doctors and others unable to participate in online events.

When developing learning solutions, WLP professionals often know the constraints and need to apply their expertise in crafting the right solutions—often a blend—to meet the business objectives and learner performance outcomes.

For example, you may have $100,000 to develop and deliver an effective training program to a group of sales representatives. Perhaps you have three months to develop the program before you need to begin delivering the training and the sales representatives are spread all across the United States. You've also found out from management that the learners will be expected to attend a kickoff call (in which you'll have 15 minutes to "plug" the program and training they'll receive), that the learners will be expected to take the training on their own after hours (so as not to cut into selling time in the field), and that their manager will be the primary go-to person and coach for any questions. All of these givens (budget, timeframe, geographically dispersed audience, and the fact that the manager is to act as the trainer if questions arise) drive the instructional design approach, the instructional strategy, and the technologies that will be selected to craft the right solution.

As mentioned previously, technology-based learning solutions are relatively new within many organizations. As a result, the last step in the process after designing and developing any technology-based learning should include capturing successes and lessons learned. As learning functions implement more and more technology-based solutions, WLP professionals need to establish a process, if one does not currently exist, to collect the best practices to make strides with regard to technology. This step helps to avoid reinventing the wheel each time a technology-based solution needs to be designed and developed in the organization.

Using Technology-Based Solutions

As technology plays a bigger role in training and learning, it is incumbent on WLP professionals to become learning-technology literate and develop a vision for how and when to apply it for specific purposes and objectives.

One barrier to understanding technology is the sheer volume of learning technologies available. In fact, there are more than 500 companies that provide learning technology solutions today across multiple categories. Development tools, collaboration tools, and the considerations that go along with each of these categories of tools all fall into the mix when designing effective technology-enabled instruction.

Development Tools

Development tools are software applications that enable WLP professionals to create learning content, without requiring previous programming skills, that can be delivered and tracked online. Keep in mind that not all development tools are designed for the same purpose. Some can be used to create both websites and online learning, while others are used to create time-based animations. Some convert Microsoft PowerPoint presentations to online courses, and still others allow the use of templates to create highly interactive simulations. Studies have indicated that most companies use multiple ***authoring tools***, selecting the right tool for the job.

Within this general category of development tools, there are specific types of tools available to WLP professionals including authoring (general purpose course authoring), rapid-development tools, simulations, instructional games, and assessment tools.

Authoring and Rapid-Development Tools

The practice of using authoring tools has been around since early computer-based training (CBT) times and these tools have evolved and are now usually delivered over the Internet.

Consider how the dynamic of shifting learning delivery formats affects the skill sets required by WLP professionals. In the early days of technology-delivered learning, when only a small percentage of training was delivered via CBT, there was often a clear delineation between those who designed instruction and those who coded, assembled, and authored courses using technology. These early technology-based courses often took a long time to develop and were costly.

With today's authoring tools, the costs and timeline to develop technology-based learning have decreased, as shown in table 4-4.

Even though authoring tools are targeted to the nonprogrammer, many authoring tools still have a steep learning curve. They allow for considerable flexibility in creating high degrees of interactivity. Studies indicate that it takes 220 person-hours of development to create a single hour of finished e-learning content. Vendors have been working to shorten development times, making authoring easier for nontechnical content contributors, and making learning development more cost effective. Some rapid-development tools allow novice developers, instructors, and ***subject matter experts (SMEs)*** to work in familiar tools, such as PowerPoint, to create learning content by converting the PowerPoint files into online courses complete with narration and interactivity.

A survey of rapid-development tool users suggests a dramatic savings in development time: 33 person-hours for each finished hour of course content created, a significant

Table 4-4. Authoring Tools Summary

Advantages	Disadvantages
• They are inexpensive and reliable. • They enable worldwide distribution.	• Materials require frequent maintenance to ensure that they're kept up to date. • They may have steep learning curves.

Source: Goldsmith (2000).

reduction from the 220:1 ratio when creating traditional technology-based content. Although rapid-development is not suitable for all types of learning content, many achieve the best results by using these rapid-development tools and mixing them with the rich interactivity of other applications, such as Flash exercises or simulations.

Collaboration Tools

What is *collaborative learning*? According to Rosenberg (2008), there are two ways to look at it. The first is more formal. WLP professionals build collaborative experiences into formal courseware in the form of group work, case studies, and other active learning approaches. There is no doubt that such techniques enhance the learning experience, but the collaborative learning discussed here doesn't necessarily happen in the context of a course or a classroom; it happens informally in the context of the workplace, driven by the individual's or group's immediate need to connect to others to answer a question, assess a situation, solve a problem, or develop a solution.

Informal learning is a requirement for organizations to remain competitive today. Learning functions need to transform themselves from being the main distributor of information in the form of training courses to one where employees have greater stewardship in their own learning.

Information flows in an organization are often chaotic. Making the problem worse is the fact that knowledge seekers, in their continued search for help, find neither the expert nor the nonexpert, but the "false" expert—the person who believes he or she has the right information but in fact is unknowingly misinformed.

One of the best ways to facilitate this transformation and empowerment of learners is through the many tools and technologies that create support for informal learning, including knowledge bases or newer Web 2.0 technologies such as wikis, blogs, discussion groups, and online communities. These Web 2.0 technologies are often low cost or free and easy to deploy.

In the late 1990s, Web 1.0 emerged and was primarily one way and informational in nature. Massive amounts of information became readily available. Today, almost 80 percent of American adults are online and have become comfortable with the Internet as a primary information source. We now see the emergence of Web 2.0, not just a technology, but a significant change in direction, characterized by dynamic person-to-person and group-to-group interactions (for example, LinkedIn and Facebook). These interactions are driving the transformation of technology-based learning into much more of an instantaneous and collaborative experience.

Collaboration tools may be one of the most important technologies in support of informal learning today. These systems are designed to capture and share expert knowledge through frequently asked questions, discussion groups, knowledge bases, or direct contact with experts via chat or instant messaging capabilities. Some examples of technologies in this category include communities of practice (CoPs), social networking, wikis, and blogs.

Communities of Practice

CoPs can serve as organizing structures and platforms for entire workplace-based learning efforts. CoPs are trusting groups of professionals united by a common concern or purpose, dedicated to supporting each other in increasing their knowledge, creating new insights, and enhancing performance in a particular domain. Members of a CoP are people who want to work with, learn from, and help each other achieve business goals (Biech 2008). Much more than chat rooms or discussion threads, CoPs are more fully integrated into actual work. Many people have been part of vertical CoPs for decades, just look at any organizational chart. In vertical CoPs, information flows up or down, but the biggest value to be gained from communities is when they are horizontal, where the information flows from side to side.

Most recently, CoPs have become associated with knowledge management as people now see them as ways of developing social capital, nurturing new knowledge, stimulating innovation, or sharing existing tacit knowledge within an organization. It is now an accepted part of organizational development.

The argument against communities is that no one uses them, especially on a regular basis. However, this issue is just as much of a cultural and sponsorship issue as it is a technology issue. CoPs flourish when members think their time is spent wisely and is valued by their peers and managers. So, communities must provide content that is deemed critical and important to members now, not at some point in the future.

Social Networking

Social networking lies at the very core of collaborative learning. John Seely Brown, former chief scientist at Xerox, first popularized the idea that learning and information sharing are social activities. People learn much more from each other than they do from more explicit information in books, magazines, websites, or videos. Adding social networking to CoPs ensures that conversations become more informal and personal, just like they are among friends and colleagues in the workplace. Tools like LinkedIn, Facebook, and MySpace are the most popular social networking sites. According to ComScore.com, Facebook and MySpace combined had approximately 166 million visitors in the last year.

Online social networks can be extensions of personal networks in the workplace, or they can focus on personal interest areas outside of work. When people can easily find others with common experience and expertise, shared knowledge can be significantly increased. The ability to instantly reach out to people with similar interests and knowledge is a powerful force in collaborative learning.

Talking about shared problems and common goals and helping others improve performance are important first steps in building a collaborative learning environment on the web.

Wikis

Wikis are generating a great deal of excitement in learning circles. A wiki (Hawaiian for quick) is a software tool that supports collaborative knowledge creation. Wikis allow groups of people to contribute and edit content in a knowledge base that has been defined and structured by a group, practically in real time, without the need for any programming knowledge. The most popular wiki by far is Wikipedia, the online encyclopedia, where almost anyone can contribute, edit, and manage information.

Wikis are based on both group-think and individual expert modules where a wide variety of participants can help to ensure that, as the group authors and edits content over time, all perspectives and points of view are heard. In addition, individual experts can evaluate and edit the content to ensure accuracy and completeness. This group collaboration, in addition to being a learning activity on its own, can serve as a collective intelligence around a particular knowledge domain.

Wikis present a group opportunity for communities of people to create knowledge bases in short order. Project teams, SMEs, market managers, and other groups of workers are often spread out geographically and can quickly use wiki technology to create and maintain repositories of information.

Blogs

Blogs, short for "weblogs," are online diaries or web journals that allow authors (bloggers) to easily and quickly communicate with large numbers of readers who then collaborate with the author by adding comments, links, and other insights and material that might be useful to the conversation. In 2006, 14 million blogs were launched, and there are an estimated 70 million blogs worldwide. Blogs are extremely easy to create and maintain; like wikis, no authoring or HTML expertise is required, just the desire to communicate and share knowledge. Unlike a wiki, a blog is usually authored by a single individual, and its format is almost always chronological.

Blogs can be powerful learning tools. They can maximize how new ideas are disseminated and discussed by a larger audience. Although it is important to ensure that those doing the blogging know what they are talking about, there is no need to restrict blogs to just a few anointed SMEs. Project managers can use a blog to keep teams, or even entire organizations, informed about a project's status. Much better than email updates, blogs form a permanent, organized record of activities and progress that can be archived and referenced. WLP professionals can use blogs to chronicle course activities that they are facilitating, perhaps over multiple offerings, in which insights from one course would not be lost to the next.

Considerations Related to Technology-Based Solutions

Although these new technologies pose exciting opportunities to enhance workplace collaboration and learning, there are several considerations to keep in mind during the selection, design, and development of technology-based learning. Some considerations are the authoring tool learning curve, the cost, how it will integrate with other systems, the mistake of assuming learners know how to use the technology, compatibility with learning management systems (LMSs) or portal technology, and different workstation configurations.

Authoring Tool Learning Curve

Authoring tools have made it more realistic for more WLP professionals to create their own learning content, unlike the days when technology experts had to code and program e-learning courses. There is still a learning curve associated with all technologies used in designing and developing learning programs today.

Cost

Many of the Web 2.0 tools may be relatively inexpensive, but authoring, rapid-development, and other development tools can come with some steep price tags if you are purchasing multiple licenses for these technologies.

Integration With Other Systems

Another consideration with regard to technology-based solutions includes integration with other systems. For example, when designing and developing content using a development tool, it is critical to understand the environment where the content will eventually live (i.e., an LMS or portal) and the specifications of the learners' computers to uncover all technical requirements early in the process and ensure that there are no compatibility issues when implementing the learning program.

Assuming That Learners Can Use Technology-Based Learning Solutions

We'd like to think that the long hours devoted to designing and developing comprehensive learning programs provide all the guidance needed for learners to access and navigate within the programs. No matter how much WLP professionals love and admire their compelling technology-based programs, if the learners find the content difficult to find and use, they will not spend time to figure it out. Today's content often has glossaries, file attachments, FAQs, narration scripts, progress quizzes, software simulations, games, interactive exercises, and more. Be sure to provide instructions on how to log on to a portal or LMS (where the content is housed), how to access and navigate the content, as well as pointing learners to all of the relevant performance support systems and *job aids* that will help them with their tasks on the job.

Compatibility With LMS or Portal Technology

If your content needs to run within a portal or LMS, it isn't prudent to assume that it will work perfectly when added to the site. Work with the LMS administrator or other resources to determine the publishing settings, publish a prototype early in the process, and then test it to ensure that the content runs without freezing up or causing any other technical glitches. Be sure to test the content from the end-user perspective to gather and communicate any setting changes that individual learners may need to make for the content to play optimally in their environment.

Workstation Configurations

Your content runs fine in any web browser, but don't assume that it will work perfectly with every learner's workstation configuration. In the technology-based learning world, learners across different departments or hierarchies may have different computers, laptops, resolutions, settings, browsers, Flash versions, and audio capabilities (some may have sound cards and others may not). Take time to work with the IT team to determine workstation configurations for the primary target audience for the technology-based learning.

Keep in mind that no matter the combination of blended learning solutions and technologies used to create a learning program, the learning must enhance performance and support the organizational strategy or else it is all for nothing.

Finally, it is critical to know the culture of the organization. When great learning initiatives, especially ones that are new and different, are pitted against an unsupportive organizational culture, the culture wins every time. If people are resistant to knowledge sharing and if collaboration is almost always forced, then it would be prudent to focus on improving the learning culture first before beginning a new and unique learning program.

Deliver/Implement/Deploy

As with any new application or technology in an organization, adoption is the key to its ultimate success. In many companies in the early to mid-1990s, there were rampant and often heated discussions about whether or not to implement email systems in organizations. People asked many questions: What is email? Why would we ever need email? Should we just give email access to management? Should we just give email access to management's administrative staff? How are we ever going to train everyone on such a potentially large enterprise application?

These questions get answered after implementation and through real-life implementation activities, but they are representative of similar questions that arise with any new technology adoption in any company. Even though there were questions when these systems were implemented, these same organizations would most likely feel completely unprepared for daily work without email connectivity.

Often, when people or organizations have issues about technology efficacy, they often stem from a lack of skills or a perceived lack of skills, which minimizes the likelihood that people will want to use these tools. This can be overcome with appropriate training, management support, and technology updates.

E-Learning

E-learning refers to anything delivered, enabled, or mediated by electronic technology for the explicit purpose of learning. E-learning allows trainers to hold classes in much the same way they would in the classroom, with a few additional considerations related to the technology. E-learning uses technology as part of the delivery process. CBT, CD-ROMs, DVDs, videos, learning portals or online communities, virtual classrooms, message boards, chat rooms, and podcasts are all examples of types of e-learning that are distributed many ways to learners.

E-learning can be placed in one of two categories: learning that occurs with a live instructor (synchronous) and learning that does not (asynchronous).

Advancements in real-time, web-based technologies have made synchronous learning possible through virtual classrooms, where participants can have a classroom learning experience without getting together in one place.

Virtual classrooms reap the benefits of traditional classroom instruction without incurring the usual costs and inconveniences (facilities, travel expenses, and so forth). Other benefits include the ability to see and hear the instructor and other participants when audio and video are used, the ability to use an unlimited number of whiteboards and to save whiteboard content automatically to use in other sessions, live online demonstrations by sharing applications, and facilitated interaction.

Other synchronous options enable learners to participate in three-dimensional virtual worlds, like Second Life. Second Life is a virtual world where users, called residents, interact with each other through avatars, which are a virtual representations of users. Residents can explore, meet other residents, socialize, participate in individual and group activities, and create and trade virtual property and services with one another, or travel throughout the world, which residents refer to as the grid.

Asynchronous learning, also called self-paced or self-directed learning, is where an instructor doesn't interact with the learner simultaneously. Using email is one form of asynchronous training. The greatest benefit of asynchronous training is its flexibility; learners can fit the course into their schedules rather than the instructor's.

E-learning also includes learner-to-learner interactions, which might occur in an online learning community, for example discussion groups, onscreen guided tours and workbooks, learning games, telementoring, and e-coaching.

Table 4-5 summarizes the advantages and disadvantages of e-learning.

Pairing Instructional and Presentation Methods

A key to gaining buy-in for technology-based solutions within the organization is to ensure that the right instructional methods have been appropriately paired with effective presentation formats to clearly communicate content, engage learners, and achieve the desired outcomes. A key goal includes engaging learners' senses by using a variety of presentation methods that cater to various adult learning and intake styles.

Table 4-5. E-Learning Summary

Advantages	Disadvantages
E-learning • gives the learner control • is outstanding for teaching rote skills because slower learners receive more remediation • is excellent for teaching prerequisite materials • allows ease of updating content in one place on the web as opposed to hundreds of CDs • offers flexibility in scheduling • is delivered quickly • requires no travel.	E-learning • requires a computer • requires a moderate to high degree of computer literacy • may have steep startup costs if no technical infrastructure is in place or the infrastructure is outdated • may be resisted by employees • decreases human contact.

As technology continues to evolve, so do instructional design techniques to more effectively pair the appropriate instructional and presentation methods. WLP professionals need to understand that technology should be selected based on the content and learning objectives and not the other way around.

The key benefits of audio and video go back to the fundamentals of cognitive learning theory. ***Multisensory learning*** engages the learner and increases retention. Audio and video can often convey feelings and subtle contexts of learning more effectively than other tools. Video is particularly effective in demonstrating a kinesthetic task, such as a tennis serve or the correct turning procedure for a bolt assembly.

There are two basic techniques—downloadable and streaming—when using audio and video content in a learning solution. Downloadable audio and video files are sent to a user's computer in their entirety before they can be played. With streaming formats, audio or video content can be played as it is being downloaded, with only a short delay at the beginning.

The advent of podcasts have made the use of audio and video more cost effective and prevalent, but audio and video are not always used. Why? A number of factors must be considered, including equipment, logistics, and extra time and cost. Even with compression techniques that make audio and video as small as possible while maintaining sound and image quality, network resources are often strained by using audio and video. When incorporating sound or images in e-learning instruction, WLP professionals must also be aware of copyright issues. More on copyright, fair use, and other legal issues is covered in chapter 15, "Legal, Regulatory, and Ethical Requirements."

Table 4-6 summarizes the advantages and disadvantages of audio and video.

Adding audio, video, and kinesthetic elements to technology-based learning is great from the learner perspective, but WLP professionals have to operate within the con-

Table 4-6. Audio and Video Summary

Advantages	Disadvantages
Audio and video • enable multisensory learning, which engages the learner and increases retention • allow WLP professionals to leverage a large library of existing audio or video training content.	Audio and video • have equipment and logistical considerations, such as required hardware (a sound card and speakers) and bandwidth restrictions • require money and time to develop.

Source: Adapted from Metcalf (2000).

straints of the organization's perspective as well. Perhaps the network does not have enough bandwidth to effectively stream audio and video in programs for the learners, it is too cost prohibitive, or adding these elements requires more time than is available to craft and deliver the training. More information on using audio and video is covered in Module 2, *Delivering Training*, chapter 4, "Training Delivery Options and Media."

Selecting Appropriate Distribution Methods

It might be surprising to some to find out that distance learning is not a new concept—formal distance learning in the United States can be historically traced as far back as the first half of the 19th century. The introduction of every new communication medium seemed to be fast, followed by the desire to use it to distribute education in a nontraditional manner. As early as 1913, Thomas Edison was forecasting the demise of traditional education models, asserting that "it is possible to teach every branch of human knowledge with the motion picture" and that "books will soon be obsolete in the public schools."

Although technology innovators like Edison have always been certain that their latest contributions to the media field are the best way to get education to everyone, everywhere, and at anytime, technology alone wasn't the answer. Educators soon realized that using the media for instructional purposes required special instructional design considerations that were different from mainstream applications of the media.

Technology-based training uses electronic technologies to deliver information and facilitate the development of skills and knowledge. To be effective in the role of a training manager, WLP professionals need to be aware of available technologies and their advantages and disadvantages. They don't need to be able to design or program these technologies but should be able to work effectively with e-learning designers and programmers, use the correct terminology, and understand the potential uses of each solution. Many technology-based solutions discussed in this chapter have overlapping uses, definitions, and terminology, which reflect ongoing debates about these terms in the WLP industry.

Evolution of Modern Educational Technologies

Generation 1: 1840s—First correspondence study via mail (shorthand)

Generation 2: 1900s—Audio recordings

Generation 3: 1910s—Motion picture camera

Generation 4: 1920s—Radio stations

Generation 5: 1930s—Television

Generation 6: 1960s—Satellite

Generation 7: 1980s—Fiber optic, audiovisual technology, CD-ROM

Generation 8: 1990s—World Wide Web, email

Generation 9: 2000s—E-learning, virtual learning, mobile learning, blogs, wikis, discussion forums, and online communities

Source: Biech (2008).

Learning technologies offer a wide variety of distribution methods including

- web-based (e-learning, learning portals, online communities, web conferencing)
- network-based (e-learning, email, collaborative tools)
- disc-based (DVD/CD-ROM)
- simulations and *virtual reality* (including tactile gear)
- mobile learning (PDA- and phone-based)
- TV-based (satellite, teleconferencing, cable)
- EPSSs
- job aids.

When considering options for learning technologies, WLP professionals should be aware of the advantages and disadvantages of various distribution methods, both in terms of the benefits they provide to learners and the organization, as well as costs and resource requirements.

Web-Based

The Internet, intranets, learning portals, online communities, bulletin boards, email communication, online courses and reference manuals, and live web conferencing enable organizations to create an electronic campus where a learner can navigate to interact with other learners, instructors, reference materials, and training sessions. Unlike a university campus, which is limited to a collection of buildings at one location, an electronic campus may have resources separated by thousands of miles.

An important difference between an intranet and the Internet is their reach. The Internet has a worldwide scope and can be traversed by anyone who can access it through a computer. Intranets, however, are usually intended for a restricted audience—those who have authorized access, usually employees of the organization that owns the intranet. An intranet may be connected to the Internet so that employees can have access to information from the Internet. However, a firewall, which is a computer security system, prevents external organizations or users from accessing the intranet.

Table 4-7 summarizes the advantages and disadvantages of web-based training (WBT).

Table 4-7. Web-Based Summary

Advantages	Disadvantages
WBT • is available from many online libraries • enables content owners to readily update materials • has low distribution costs • enables learners to access multiple courses on a single piece of web software • allows self-paced training.	WBT • requires a computer • requires a moderate to high degree of computer literacy to create WBT sites • may have bandwidth issues, especially when content includes sound and streaming video • offers limited video and sound transmission • requires security measures to prevent unwanted viewing.

Network-Based

Many organizations provide training and content to learners via their corporate network. Corporate networks often provide one-stop shopping for learners to access anytime, anywhere learning from one key point.

One benefit of providing network-based learning solutions includes a reduced distribution cost. With disc-based delivery methods, discs need to be made for each learner, then delivered. Network-based learning skirts the challenges and additional cost of disc-based distribution.

Corporate networks, however, often have bandwidth restrictions. Content developed to be delivered via a network may need to be limited with regard to the amount of audio, video, interactivity, or the final size of the e-learning content to meet the IT guidelines and standards for delivering content this way. Table 4-8 summarizes the advantages and disadvantages of network-based training.

Disc-Based

CBT content can also be distributed to learners via disc-based methods (primarily DVDs and CD-ROMs). CD-ROM, an initialism of Compact Disc Read-Only Memory, is a pre-

Table 4-8. Network-Based Summary

Advantages	Disadvantages
Network-based training	Network-based training
• is available to learners through a wide variety of content • can be distributed quickly to numerous locations • eliminates concerns about scheduling constraints • allows self-paced training • has low distribution costs and evaluation built into the instruction • enables use of existing videos and visuals.	• requires a computer • may have high development costs and lengthy development timelines • requires moderate computer literacy of users • may not be appropriate for learners with low self-directedness • may be constrained by amount of audio, video, and interactivity that is included in the content due to bandwidth or other IT restrictions.

pressed CD that contains data accessible to, but not writable by, a computer. The CD format was originally designed for music storage and playback. When DVD arrived, it quickly became the most popular disc-based media format.

DVDs, also known as Digital Versatile Discs or Digital Video Discs, have the same dimensions as CDs but store more than six times as much data. The large storage capacity enables many organizations to take advantage of learning solutions that don't require learners to go online. For example, some organizations may have size limitations on courses that can live on the LMS. For courses or learning programs that are too large because of large amounts of audio and video, the learning content can be distributed to learners on a disc rather than via the Internet or intranet.

Table 4-9 summarizes the advantages and disadvantages of disc-based training.

Simulators and Virtual Reality

Ask any group of WLP professionals to define the word *simulation,* and you're likely to get a wide variety of answers. Educational simulations are a broad genre of simulations that focus on increasing participants' mastery level in the real world.

Educational simulations use simulation elements to model and present an abstracted reality, including

- real-life or target actions reflected in the interface

- how the actions then affect relevant systems, including any units, maps, and work processes

- how those systems produce feedback and results.

The simulation elements are then mixed with game elements to make it engaging. The addition of pedagogical elements, including coaching, make it effective.

Table 4-9. Disc-Based Summary

Advantages	Disadvantages
Disc-based training • allows for larger courses and content without LMS or bandwidth restrictions • eliminates concerns about scheduling constraints • allows self-paced training • has evaluation built into the instruction • enables use of existing videos and visuals.	Disc-based training • is not as easily distributed as network- or web-based distribution methods • has higher distribution costs compared to web- and network-based distribution methods • requires a computer • may have high development costs • may require lengthy development timelines • may not be appropriate for learners with low self-directedness.

Simulations are also organized into tasks and levels to create incrementally challenging practice environments and can be engaged by one or more participants and often surrounded by a community.

Once understood, different genres of simulations make creating and using simulations much easier and more predictable.

Genre 1: Branching Stories

A branching story is an educational simulation genre in which learners make a series of multiple-choice decisions to progress through and affect an event. Specifically, learners start with a briefing, then they advance to a first multiple-choice decision point (or branch). Based on the decision or action they make, they see a scene that provides some feedback, advances the story, and then sets up another decision. Learners continue making decisions, traversing some of the available branches, until they either win or lose by reaching a successful or unsuccessful final state. Finally, learners get some type of after-action review.

Genre 2: Interactive Spreadsheets

Another popular genre of educational simulation is the interactive spreadsheet. This is an educational simulation in which learners typically try to affect three or four critical metrics indirectly and over time by allocating finite resources along competing categories over a series of turns or intervals. Learners get feedback on their decisions through graphs and charts after each interval. The entire simulation might continue for between three and 20 intervals.

These interactive spreadsheets are often used in a multiplayer or team-based environment with significant competition among learners and often with a coach or facilitator to help.

Genre 3: The Virtual Lab

The third genre is virtual labs, in which learners are given realistic, online versions of objects or applications and are given challenges to solve. For example, automotive dealers might be given a smoking car. They have to find the right tools, such as a diagnostic computer terminal, pop the hood by pressing the right buttons, attach the cable to the right spot in the engine, and start the computer by pressing the right sequence of buttons. What learners do, where they do it, how hard they do it, and how long they press the "turn wrench" button all matter, which means that there is much kinesthetic learning going on.

Genre 4: Minigames

The final popular genre of simulations is called minigames. Minigames, also called casual games or microgames, are easy to access, are most often Adobe Flash–based, and represent between five and 20 minutes of learner engagement. Minigames are fun (quick gameplay, bouncy music, and appealing graphics) and educational. This genre is perfect for skills or activities that need repetition and practice.

Naturally, cost is always a deciding factor. The costs for these technologies have decreased in recent years, such that simulations are becoming relatively affordable.

Virtual reality (VR) is a computer-based technology that gives learners a realistic, three-dimensional, interactive experience. This powerful tool enhances learning by allowing students to perform skills in a realistic, engaging simulation of a real-life environment. Like other types of e-learning, VR can reduce average learning time and, therefore, the cost associated with learning. Many organizations use VR to deliver performance-based learning solutions.

Authors Mohr, Field, and Frank (2000) point out in *The ASTD Handbook of Training Design and Delivery* that VR is inherently a self-directed and self-paced experience. A single learner, immersed in a virtual environment, interacts with surrounding objects, and then experiences the results of those actions through visual, aural, and sometimes tactile feedback. VR is often applied to simulation or scenario-based learning applications that enable learners to perform skills and apply knowledge while working at their own pace. It can be used in self-paced learning, instructor-led learning, and other learning methods, depending on factors such as cost, time to delivery, learning content, and learners.

VR-based, self-paced programs are most effective for teaching cognitive or procedural skills. These programs can be designed for orientation for new staff, refresher/remedial instruction for experienced staff, and skill practice and rehearsal for all staff. VR shares the benefits of other CBT technologies, but some specific benefits and disadvantages are listed in table 4-10.

TV-Based (Satellite, Teleconferencing, and Cable)

Businesses have used video teleconferencing for several years in lieu of face-to-face meetings, primarily in a small number of sites. However, it has become one of the most

Table 4-10. Simulation-Based Summary

Advantages	Disadvantages
Simulator-based	Simulator-based
• engages learners in the learning experience and increases their motivation to learn • provides a wide variety of realistic conditions and feedback from practicing and rehearsing skills in a safe, risk-free environment • promotes conceptual and procedural learning tasks • reduces errors in performing skills, particularly for complex tasks • increases retention.	• requires an initial investment in hardware and software that may be cost prohibitive • requires a detailed understanding of cause and effect • requires a number of resources for developing and delivering learning applications • may need specialized equipment depending on requirements for the type of interaction.

Source: Adapted from Mohr, Field, and Frank (2000).

common methods of training at a distance. Learners can see and hear the instructor, and the instructor can see and hear learners. Video teleconferencing is sometimes referred to as "two way, two way," referring to the two-way transmission of both audio and video signals.

With video teleconferencing, the equipment is often the same at both the instructor site (or source site) and the learner site (or remote site). Having the same equipment offers the flexibility for any site in the system to become an instructor site. Typically, equipment in a video teleconferencing classroom includes

- *Cameras:* Cameras at each site capture what the instructor and learners are doing. The setup usually includes three cameras: one oriented toward where an instructor sits, a second overhead camera directed at where an instructor places visual aids (paper, slides, or three-dimensional objects), and a third camera pointed where learners sit. The cameras can be controlled by those physically at the site or by someone at a remote site.

- *Remote control:* A remote control, similar to that for a television or video recorder, allows an instructor or a learner to choose which camera is displayed and control the camera's angle and zoom. Other devices to control cameras include one that zooms in automatically on whoever is talking.

- **Codec:** A camera's video signal is fed to the "brains" of the site, an electronic box called a codec (short for coder/decoder). The codec converts the camera signal, along with audio signals from classroom microphones into digital information. The information is then sent, usually over high-capacity phone lines, to remote sites. After remote sites have received the digital information, the codec at each site converts the digital signal back to a signal that can be displayed on a television monitor.

- *Television monitors:* Two large television monitors allow participants to see both what cameras at their own site (outgoing video) are seeing and what cameras at the remote site (incoming video) are seeing.

Other audiovisual sources can be linked to the codec. Most sites are equipped with a video recorder so the instructor can transmit a videotape signal to the other sites. A special type of 35mm slide projector commonly used at video teleconference sites displays slides as video signals that are fed into the codec, not as images that go through a lens to a wall or screen. With this technology, existing 35mm slides can be used during an instruction or training period.

Table 4-11 summarizes the advantages and disadvantages of TV-based training.

Mobile Learning

One of the latest trends in distance learning is mobile learning. According to the Learning Mobile Citizen, mobile learning is "the use of mobile or wireless devices for learning on the move." Mobile learning provides curricula where and when you need it, using delivery technologies that enable learners to carry learning with them.

Technologies in this category include MP3 players, pocket PCs, mobile phones, and personal digital assistants (PDAs). PDA-based learning delivery includes podcasts (audio) and vodcasts (video). There are certainly many other miniature devices that will fall into this category, not to mention the combination of technologies to create new learning devices. The launch of the Apple iPhone is an example of the convergence of these technologies, as consumers are becoming less willing to carry around multiple devices. As this convergence continues, the types and amounts of instruction that will be delivered via mobile learning will exponentially explode.

This delivery method represents a new take on old technology. What was once sent out on audiocassettes, videotapes, and CD-ROMs/DVDs is now downloaded directly off the Internet or a local hard drive. Along with easier-to-use production tools, the ability to distribute a wide variety of audiovisual material over the Internet has made the podcast

Table 4-11. TV-Based Summary

Advantages	Disadvantages
TV-based training • allows instructors to see learners (and vice versa) • offers the flexibility of multiple "instructor" sites • enables learners to interact with each other visually.	TV-based training • has high transmission costs • has high costs for establishing sites • presents difficulties in managing visual interaction with several sites.

Source: Mantyla and Dividen (1997).

and all of its cousins extremely popular and far less costly than past approaches. Another contribution of the podcast is that it has transformed the traditional perceptions of what a knowledge base is.

Ultimately, mobile learning is convenient. Learning can occur when you need it (just-in-time) and, in theory, from wherever you happen to be.

For example, do you need to know how to fix a pressure gauge on an agricultural vehicle when you are 20 miles away from the office? Use a PDA to help guide you through the steps. Learning a new language? Listen to a podcast with headphones while commuting on the train. Watching a how-to video on an MP3 player with video capability and missed a step? Simply rewind and watch again.

Table 4-12 summarizes the advantages and disadvantages of mobile learning.

Mobile devices and podcasts have grown in number and sophistication. This technology is a no-brainer in knowledge dissemination and learning as it offers the user the ability to learn on the go, from experts who otherwise would have a more limited reach, and to get updates to the content every day if desired (if synched with a computer).

Electronic Performance Support Systems

An EPSS is a software program that provides just-in-time, on-demand information, guidance, examples, and step-by-step dialog boxes to improve job performance without the need for training or coaching by other people. An EPSS is, in other words, a comprehensive computer-based job aid.

EPSS applications often include

- databases of job-related information organized to facilitate rapid access and optimize clarity

- calculators and wizards that simplify and automate procedures

- decision-support modules that offer intelligent assistance with problem solving

- embedded tutorials and simulations that provide instruction in work-related concepts and procedures.

A well-designed EPSS is more than an electronic page turner or multimedia document. It incorporates the decision support of expert systems, the information accessibility of

Table 4-12. Mobile Learning Summary

Advantages	Disadvantages
Mobile learning • is inexpensive to create • does not require high-end skills to create content • is easy to use and low cost.	Mobile learning • has limited or no use of graphics • contains the potential trap of quickly creating content without thought to instructional design.

electronic text retrieval systems, and the individualized instructional capabilities of CBT or WBT. It can even include advanced communication features.

An EPSS—or any job aid for that matter—addresses the same performance needs as training. In fact, when performers lack the knowledge or skills required to perform the job at hand, only two possible solutions work: training and job aids. Of course, performance opportunities aren't generally either/or situations; training and job aids are often used together as complementary solutions.

EPSSs are best used for noncomplex tasks. If learners have to make too many decisions within steps, they may get lost. Table 4-13 summarizes the advantages and disadvantages of EPSSs.

Table 4-13. EPSS Summary

Advantages	Disadvantages
EPSSs • allow self-paced training • have low distribution costs • can be used to address a performance problem caused by a knowledge or skill deficiency.	EPSSs • require a computer • may not be an appropriate training solution for psychomotor tasks • may need extensive employee and organizational commitment to keep procedures and other information up-to-date in the system.

Source: Adapted from Sanders and Thiagarajan (2001).

Job Aids

A job aid (sometimes also called a "cheat sheet") is a storage place for information on how to perform a specific task. A job aid provides an audio or visual signal to a performer about when to carry out a task and steps, reducing the amount of recall that's needed and minimizing error. In everyday life, people use job aids when they are at an ATM or a self-service gas pump, for example.

Job aids reduce training time and support learning. For example, in a commercial airplane, pilots use job aids (preflight checklists) to make sure they carry out vital tasks to ensure safe flights. The key to creating good job aids is to organize the information according to how users will actually use it, step by step. For more on developing and using job aids, refer to Module 2, *Delivering Training*, chapter 4, "Training Delivery Options and Media." Table 4-14 summarizes the advantages and disadvantages of job aids.

Types of Organizational Knowledge Management Systems

Technology serves as an enabler to allow organizations to capture, store, retrieve, and share knowledge among members. Many organizations use several ways to share knowledge via content management systems (CMSs), websites, and intranet portals. Several types of knowledge management systems include the following:

Table 4-14. Job Aids Summary

Advantages	Disadvantages
Job aids • are excellent for tasks performed with low frequency, highly complex tasks, tasks with a high consequence of error, and tasks likely to change in the future • can be used as "checklists" when a series of tasks or checkpoints must be completed in a certain order every time, for example, a preflight checklist that must be done before takeoff.	Job aids • can't be used for tasks that have strict time restrictions, such as tasks a pilot must perform midflight when immediate reaction times are crucial • aren't practical for use in some environments; for example, a scuba diver can't handle a booklet in dark, wet conditions.

Source: Adapted from Sanders and Thiagarajan (2005).

A *CMS* is a computer software system for organizing and facilitating collaborative creation of documents and other content. It is often a web application used for managing websites and web content, though, in many cases, CMSs require special client software for editing and constructing articles.

A *learning content management system (LCMS)* applies the primary functions of content management—storing, searching for, and reusing content—to the training development process. In an LCMS, content is chunked (typically into *learning objects*, which are small, reusable pieces of content) and then managed, published, and delivered on demand. LCMSs integrate different courses and learning materials and then package the content for print, DVD, or electronic publication. Most are capable of importing prepackaged content from other learning content development tools, such as Microsoft Word and Macromedia Dreamweaver. Most LCMSs enable course developers to author learning content as well.

A *web portal* is a website that serves as a starting point to other resources on the Internet or an intranet. Intranet portals, also known as enterprise information portals, provide access to an array of resources and services, such as email, forums, search engines, and online shopping malls. The first web portals were online services, such as AOL. Today, many early search engines have changed into web portals to attract a larger audience. Many business portals offer collaboration services to share information in workplaces.

A *document management system* is a computer program (or set of programs) used to track and store images of paper documents. More recently, the term has been used to distinguish between imaging and records management systems that specialize in paper capture and records, respectively. Document management systems commonly offer check-in, check-out, storage, and retrieval of electronic documents. Electronic document management systems typically include a work-flow model for certifying and electronically signing documents.

Collaboration tools are software systems designed to capture and share expert knowledge through frequently asked questions, discussion groups, knowledge bases, or direct contact with experts via chat or instant messaging capabilities. Some examples of technologies in this category include wikis, social networking sites (e.g., LinkedIn, Facebook), CoPs, discussion threads, chat, and instant messaging.

Conclusion

The Internet and technology have changed everything in the world of learning. Resources, education, information, varied points of view, and CoPs are now possible wherever we are. It has enabled WLP professionals and employees to be the producers and creators of lessons, stories, and modules.

The learning technology space is evolving quickly, sometimes faster than our ability to plan how we can leverage the technology to keep pace with what learners need. Only five years ago, blogs were just making a splash and few knew what a wiki was before Wikipedia became a household name. With numerous learning technology components available, it is becoming increasingly important to keep up with what's happening in each category of the various technologies.

From the perspective of a WLP professional, these new learning technologies require several new skills and areas of expertise in addition to traditional instructional design skills. Specialties like information design, knowledge architecture design, library science, user interface design, community facilitation, collaboration strategy, content analysis, and change management are becoming increasingly important. These new technologies represent more than profound changes in the technology alone; they are transforming the implementation of organizational change. Where once WLP professionals could only provide courses to meet the learning needs of employees, they now can maintain and deliver workplace-based information and collaboration services as well.

✓ **Chapter 4 Knowledge Check**

1. **Which of the following delivery methods is best for learners with a low level of self-directedness?**

   __ **A.** VR

   __ **B.** EPSS

   __ **C.** E-learning

   __ **D.** Classroom instruction

2. **Which delivery method has the primary advantages of being excellent for teaching rote skills and prerequisite materials, offering flexibility in scheduling, and being capable of quick delivery?**

   __ **A.** Job aids

   __ **B.** EPSS

   __ **C.** E-learning

   __ **D.** Classroom instruction

3. **A manager of a small company is trying to decide if high-end simulations are an appropriate training option to deliver new product training to salespeople. Which of the following factors makes simulations inappropriate for this company?**

   __ **A.** The company has five regional offices.

   __ **B.** The company needs to monitor postassessment scores.

   __ **C.** The training will be updated quarterly.

   __ **D.** The training must include product demonstration videos.

4. **With video teleconferencing, the equipment is often the same at both the instructor site and the learner sites, which provides the flexibility for any site in the system to become an instructor site.**

   __ **A.** True

   __ **B.** False

5. **Which of the following is *not* an advantage of a job aid?**

   __ **A.** Excellent for tasks with low frequency

   __ **B.** Excellent for tasks with short reaction time

   __ **C.** Excellent for tasks with high consequence of error

   __ **D.** Excellent for tasks likely to change in the future

6. **The benefits of audio and video in instruction include enabling multisensory learning.**

   __ **A.** True

   __ **B.** False

---

7. **A manager is reviewing the reasons for providing employees with an EPSS as a job aid. Of the following scenarios, which one is considered the best reason for using an EPSS?**

   __ **A.** Access to computers is limited.

   __ **B.** Employees require just-in-time performance assistance.

   __ **C.** Information and processes are changing constantly.

   __ **D.** The tasks are highly technical and fairly complicated.

---

8. **One of the biggest barriers to implementing technology-based learning is**

   __ **A.** Organizational culture

   __ **B.** Learner skills

   __ **C.** Mission and vision of the organization

   __ **D.** Cost

---

9. **Which of the following was created in an effort to minimize or remove technical roadblocks and fosters creation of reuseable learning content as "instructional objects"?**

   __ **A.** SCORM

   __ **B.** Section 508

   __ **C.** Blended learning

   __ **D.** Wikis

---

10. **When selecting a learning technology, the most important consideration in the selection process is**

    __ **A.** Identifying the learning objectives and desired outcomes and selecting the technology to support those goals

    __ **B.** Identifying the target audience and geographical location(s)

    __ **C.** Determining which activities and interactivity are needed

    __ **D.** Constructing a rationale for the technology choice

11. Which of the following is best defined as a term covering a wide set of applications and processes, such as virtual classrooms, digital collaboration, and so on? Delivery of content may be via the Internet/intranet/extranet (LAN/WAN), audiotape and videotape, satellite broadcast, interactive TV, CD-ROM, and more.

__ A. Podcasts

__ B. E-learning

__ C. Vodcasts

__ D. Teleconferencing

12. Video teleconferencing allows the instructor to see learners and vice versa.

__ A. True

__ B. False

13. Which of the following is best described as an exercise with a simplified form of a real-life situation so that participants can practice making decisions and analyzing results of those decisions?

__ A. Simulations

__ B. EPSSs

__ C. VR

__ D. Social networks

14. A WLP professional working in a federal government agency is instructed by his manager that the e-learning content he is researching to purchase from a vendor must be accessible by federal employees with disabilities. The standard that the manager is referencing is

__ A. SCORM

__ B. Section 508

__ C. Mobile learning standards

__ D. Collaboration tool standards

15. Which of the following is defined as a CBT that gives learners a realistic, three-dimensional, interactive experience?

__ A. Simulation

__ B. E-learning

__ C. VR

__ D. Psychomotor skills

16. **A WLP professional is creating a blended learning program and wants to leverage collaboration tools to facilitate the learning process and provide informal learning experiences for the target audience outside of formal classroom instruction. All of the following are examples of collaboration software *except***

  ___ **A.** Wikis

  ___ **B.** Blogs

  ___ **C.** CoPs

  ___ **D.** LMSs

References

Biech, E., editor. (2008). *The ASTD Handbook for Workplace Learning Professionals.* Alexandria, VA: ASTD Press.

Chapman, B. (2008). "Learning Technology Primer." *The ASTD Handbook for Workplace Learning Professionals*, E. Biech, editor. Alexandria, VA: ASTD Press.

Ellis, A.L., E.D. Wagner, and W.R. Longmire. (1999). *Managing Web-Based Training.* Alexandria, VA: ASTD Press.

Elsenheimer, J. (February 2003). "Terms of Engagement: Keeping Learners Online." *Learning Circuits.* www.learningcircuits.org/2003/feb2003 /elearn.html.

Goldsmith, J.J. (2000). "Development Teams for Creating Technology-Based Training." *The ASTD Handbook of Training Design and Delivery,* G.M. Piskurich, P. Beckschi, and B. Hall, editors. New York: McGraw-Hill.

Hartley, D.E. (July 2006). "Complex IT Infrastructures Warrant Thorough Preparation." *T&D,* pp. 21–22.

———. (November 2006.) "Catalyzing the Learning Process." *T&D,* p. 22.

Hodell, C. (2000). *ISD From the Ground Up.* Alexandria, VA: ASTD Press.

Hoffman, J., and J. Bozarth. (2008). "Distance Learning and Web-Based Training." *The ASTD Handbook for Workplace Learning Professionals*, E. Biech, editor. Alexandria, VA: ASTD Press.

Lee, A.Y., and A.N. Bowers. (1997). "The Effects of Multimedia Components on Learning." Proceedings of the Human Factors and Ergonomics Society 41st Annual Meeting, pp. 340–344.

Mantyla, K., and J.R. Gividen. (1997). *Distance Learning: A Step-by-Step Guide for Trainers.* Alexandria, VA: ASTD Press.

McArdle, G.E. (1999). *Training Design and Delivery.* Alexandria, VA: ASTD Press.

Metcalf, D.S., II. (2000). "Using Audio and Video Over the Web." *The ASTD Handbook of Training Design and Delivery*, G.M. Piskurich, P. Beckschi, and B. Hall, editors. New York: McGraw-Hill.

Mohr, C.G., S. Field, and G. Frank. (2000). "Virtual Reality: Is It for You?" *The ASTD Handbook of Training Design and Delivery,* G.M. Piskurich, P. Beckschi, and B. Hall, editors. New York: McGraw-Hill.

Oakes, K., and R. Rengarajan. (September 2002). "E-Learning: Synching Up With Virtual Classrooms." *T&D,* pp. 57–60.

Piskurich, G.M., and E.S. Sanders. (1998). *ASTD Models for Learning Technologies: Roles, Competencies, and Outputs.* Alexandria, VA: ASTD Press.

Piskurich, G.M., P. Beckschi, and B. Hall, editors. (2000). *The ASTD Handbook of Training Design and Delivery*. New York: McGraw-Hill.

Prager, H. (2008). "Managing Learning Like a Business." *The ASTD Handbook for Workplace Learning Professionals*, E. Biech, editor. Alexandria, VA: ASTD Press.

Rosenberg, M.J. (June 2008). "Technology Euphoria?" *T&D*, pp. 24–25.

———. (2008). "Learning Meets Web 2.0 Collaborative Learning." *The ASTD Handbook for Workplace Learning Professionals*, E. Biech, editor. Alexandria, VA: ASTD Press.

Rossen, E., and D.E. Hartley. (2001). "Basics of E-Learning." *Infoline* No. 250109.

Rossett, A. (February 2008). "The Long View with Allison Rossett." *T&D*, p. 83.

Rossett, A., et al. (June 2003). "Strategies for Building Blended Learning." *Learning Circuits*, www.astd.org/LC/2003/0703_rossett.htm.

Sanders, E.S., and S. Thiagarajan. (2001). *Performance Intervention Maps: 36 Strategies for Solving Your Organization's Problems*. Alexandria, VA: ASTD Press.

———. (2005). *Performance Intervention Maps: 39 Strategies for Solving Your Organization's Problems* (Revised Edition). Alexandria, VA: ASTD Press.

Simon, M. (January 2009). "E-Learning No How." *T&D*, p. 35.

Toth, T. (2003). *Technology for Trainers*. Alexandria, VA: ASTD Press.

5
Learning Information Systems

A *learning information system* is a tool that benefits training managers in program administration and the design and delivery of training. At the program administration level, learning information systems provide databases for administering training programs, which generate rosters, certificates, and registration reports. They can store templates and modules of information for building training curriculums. Learning information systems can also be used at the learner level in the classroom; through e-learning; and outside the classroom with self-paced materials, reference documents, and job aids.

Learning information systems not only support the work efforts of workplace learning and performance (WLP) professionals, but also strengthen the organization. They can facilitate learning by supporting the processes of knowledge acquisition, information distribution, information interpretation, and organizational memory.

Learning Objectives:

- ☑ Describe the purpose of different types of learning information systems, including learning management systems (LMSs), learning content management systems (LCMSs), collaboration tools, and learning support systems (LSSs)

- ☑ List the effects of LMSs and the role they play in the development of a new training department.

- ☑ List three ways learning systems may be incorporated into the learning function.

Types of Learning Information Systems

A training manager can use many learning systems to support the training function; learners; and content design, development, and delivery. Typically, WLP professionals use learning information systems for classroom learning, e-learning, and self-paced learning through reference documents. Four common types of learning information systems are

1. LMSs

2. LCMSs

3. ***collaborative learning software***

4. LSSs.

WLP professionals may have difficulty determining whether it's best to purchase an LMS, an LCMS, or both and identifying the type of collaborative learning software to choose that will support all training and learner needs. This confusion is due to the subtle, though unique, distinctions between an LMS and an LCMS. Although many vendors offer combination LCMS–LMS solutions, core differences exist between the two. An LMS manages learners (who's taking what, completion rates, course progress status, and so forth), and an LCMS manages content (the components that make up a course).

LMS Implementation

An LMS is a software application that automates administering, tracking, and reporting classroom and online training events. This automation allows detailed analysis of the effectiveness of the training investment. Organizations purchase an LMS to provide information that influences decision making and optimizes training dollars.

When organizations select and implement an LMS, two success factors must be in place. First, a corporate learning blueprint needs to exist that clearly articulates the current learning environment and the desired future state. The blueprint should be aligned with organizational learning goals and have buy-in from leadership. Second, seamless LMS integration doesn't exist, so training managers need to acknowledge the sizable costs associated with migrating databases, constructing digital connectors to other enterprise software systems, developing or migrating content, and customizing reports.

These are other assessments that should be conducted when planning to use an LMS or other learning information system:

- *Strategic analysis* identifies the organization's business objectives as they relate to workforce development, defines high-level priority targets for knowledge and skill transfer, and describes—in basic terms—the current and desired future learning environment.

- *Information technology (IT) infrastructure assessment* provides baseline information about the current configuration of the company's IT backbone and details on desktop programs across the enterprise. This assessment should define connectivity for remote learners and those closer to the central IT hubs. It should also explore internal or external hosting options. For example, if the organization hosts the LMS internally, the IT department needs to understand that the LMS requires continued support. That support translates to bandwidth and labor costs that often aren't factored into a company's investment decision. This assessment also engages the IT department at the beginning of the process and helps ensure ongoing support, which is critical to a successful LMS implementation, whether it's hosted internally or externally.

- *Cultural readiness assessment* helps determine an organization's ability to embrace new learning strategies. Often, LMS implementation projects address all of the technical aspects adequately but overlook political, cultural, and practical implications. This oversight generally results in a stalled or failed initiative. A cultural readiness assessment helps define parameters for success, such as whether an internal marketing program is needed.

- *Administrative process analysis* maps existing administrative efforts that govern the training function and identifies procedures that will change with an LMS solution, such as handling overbooked classes and capturing and recording learner results and feedback. This analysis also determines where the LMS needs to connect to existing human resources (HR) software systems and databases.

- *Internal assessment* helps an organization define its future learning blueprint, including a vision and planning effort that takes about four to six weeks.

These assessments help develop a clear picture of required functionality and create LMS bid specifications that most closely align with an organization's business needs. Some questions to consider when developing an organization's e-learning architecture are as follows:

- Will the organization or the vendor host the solution?

- Does the training department need content development tools?

- Does the organization require a competency module that helps define skills gaps for building individualized learning plans?

- Is there an e-commerce element?

- Will links be built to additional company or external information sources?

- Does a synchronous online component enable e-mentoring and creating online learning communities?

- Does the training department need online assessment capabilities?

- Will learners need to connect to external communities, such as suppliers or customers?

LMS

An *LMS* is a high-level strategic solution for planning, delivering, and managing all learning events in an organization, including online, virtual classroom, and instructor-led courses. The solution involves replacing isolated and fragmented learning programs with a systematic means of assessing and raising competency and performance levels throughout an organization. For example, an LMS simplifies global certification efforts, enables companies to align learning initiatives with strategic goals, and provides a viable means of enterprise-level skills management. The focus of an LMS is to manage learners, keeping track of their progress and performance across all types of training activities. It performs heavy-duty administrative tasks, such as reporting to HR and other enterprise resource-planning systems, but generally, it isn't used to create course content.

An LMS provides a single point of access to disparate learning sources. It automates learning program administration and offers unprecedented opportunities for HR development. It identifies the people who need a particular course and tells them how it fits into their overall career path, when it's available, how it's available (for example, classroom, online, CD-ROM), whether it has prerequisites, and when and how to fulfill prerequisites. After learners complete a course, an LMS can administer tests based on proficiency requirements, report test results, and recommend next steps. In that capacity, LMSs are instrumental in ensuring that organizations meet rigid certification and compliance requirements in vertical markets, such as healthcare, finance, and government.

An LMS should have these capabilities:

- *Support for blended learning:* Because adults learn in different ways, an LMS should offer a curriculum that mixes classroom and virtual courses easily. Combining these features enables prescriptive and personalized training.

- *Integration with HR systems:* An LMS must synchronize with HR systems for maximum effectiveness. When these systems are integrated, an HR employee can enter new employees' information into the HR system and automatically sign them up for training tailored to their roles in the company.

- *Administration tools:* An LMS must enable learning administrators to manage user registrations and profiles; define roles; set curriculums; chart certification paths; assign tutors; author courses; manage content; and administer internal budgets, user payments, and chargebacks. Administrators need complete access to the training database so that they can create standard and customized reports on individual and group performance. Reports should be scalable to include the entire workforce. The system should also be able to build schedules for learners, instructors, and classrooms. Most important, all features should be manageable by using automated user-friendly interfaces.

- *Content integration:* An LMS must be able to offer built-in support for a wide range of third-party courseware. Some LMSs are compatible only with the supplier's own courseware, and others do little more than pay lip service to learning content standards. An LMS supplier should be able to certify that third-party content works in its system, and access to courses should be as easy as using a drop-down menu.

- *Adherence to standards:* An LMS should be able to support technical standards, such as the Sharable Courseware Object Reference Model and the Airline Industry CBT Committee specification. When it supports standards, an LMS can import and manage content and courseware that complies with standards, regardless of the authoring system that produced it. WLP professionals should be aware that if the supplier doesn't certify that the content will work, additional expenses in standards compliance may be required.

- *Assessment capabilities:* Evaluation, testing, and assessment engines help build a program that becomes more valuable over time. An assessment feature that enables authoring and includes assessments as part of each course ensures that learning is measured and the learning function adds value to the organization.

- *Skills management:* A skills management component enables organizations to measure training and development needs and identify areas for improvement based on workers' collective competence. Skills assessments can be culled from multiple sources, including peer reviews and 360-degree feedback tools. Managers determine whether results are weighted, averaged, or compared to determine a skill gap. An organization also can use this feature to search its employee base for specialized skills.

LCMS

LCMSs combine the most essential pieces of the learning puzzle—namely, courses and learning materials. LCMSs package content for print, CD-ROM, or electronic publication, and most are capable of importing prepackaged content from other learning content development tools, such as Microsoft Word and Macromedia Dreamweaver. WLP professionals should know that an LCMS's capability to import content from various sources cleanly is crucial.

In addition, course developers can use LCMSs as primary authoring tools for developing learning content. Furthermore, LCMSs allow developers to manage course content in a centralized way and forgo hours of manual work by quickly reusing and reconfiguring existing course content and creating multiple courses for different purposes with the same content.

The research company IDC defines an LCMS as a system that creates, stores, assembles, and delivers personalized learning content in the form of learning objects. Though an LMS manages and administers all forms of learning within an organization, an LCMS concentrates on online learning content usually in the form of learning objectives.

A *learning object* is a self-contained chunk of instructional material. It typically includes three components: a performance goal (what the learner will understand or be able to accomplish upon completion of the instruction), the necessary learning content to reach that goal (such as text, video, illustration, bulleted slide, demo, task simulation), and some form of evaluation to measure whether the goal was achieved.

A learning object also includes metadata, or tags, to describe its content and purpose to the LCMS. Metadata may include information, such as author, language, and version level. So how are learning objects used to create content? An LCMS stores learning objects in a central repository for instructional designers to retrieve and assemble into personalized courses. This benefits developers and learners because traditional courses tend to contain more content than any single learner can absorb or needs to absorb about a topic. By breaking course content into learning objects and serving them up on an as-needed basis, content developers can deliver just-in-time and just-enough learning. The end result is increased productivity because learners are not wasting time wading through irrelevant material.

According to Hall and Hall (2004), many LCMSs offer various benefits such as these:

- *Faster development:* A what-you-see-is-what-you-get *(WYSIWYG)* authoring environment enables WLP professionals to quickly create and publish just-in-time training.

- *Collaboration:* Learning content stored in an LCMS can be checked in and checked out. In addition, LCMSs have version control. These functions enable multiple users to access and work on the same course simultaneously.

- *Reuse:* The ability to create content once and reuse it multiple times enables instructional designers to create the same content for publication in various formats. For example, content could be created for a web-based course for learners with Internet access and published in print format with learners without web access.

- *Quick global updates:* When content needs to be updated, the updates can be made to one learning objective and then published so that all instances of the objective are automatically updated throughout the LCMS.

Table 5-1, based primarily on research conducted by Brandon Hall, summarizes the differences between an LMS and an LCMS.

Collaborative Learning Software

According to Bonk (2002), collaboration, communication, and conversation can lead to a competitive advantage for organizations and for learning. Collaborative technologies (also called collaborative learning software) have emerged to offer a way to familiarize learners with new expectations and experiences. Collaboration tools include email, computer networks, whiteboards, bulletin board systems, chat rooms, and online presentation tools. These technologies play an important role in the expansion of e-learning and in collaborating on projects, sharing information, and communicating.

Although the primary goal of e-learning is knowledge transfer, collaborative learning tools can also help foster learners' analytical skills, critical thinking, and idea generation, and they can help bridge the gaps of perceived importance or practice. Bonk (2002) outlines

Table 5-1. Differences Between an LMS and an LCMS

	LMS	LCMS
Who benefits?	All learners and the organization	Content developers and learners who need personalized content
Provides primary management of?	Learning performance, learning requirements, and learning programs and planning	Learning content
Manages e-learning?	Yes	Yes
Manages traditional forms of training, such as instructor-led courses?	Yes	No
Tracks results?	Yes	Yes
Supports learner collaboration?	Yes	Yes
Includes learner profile management?	Yes	No
Allows HR and enterprise resource planning systems to share learner data?	Yes	No
Schedules events?	Yes	No
Offers competency mapping or skill gap analysis?	Yes	No
Includes registration, prerequisite screening, and cancellation notification?	Yes	No
Creates test questions and test administration?	Yes	Yes
Supports dynamic pretesting and adaptive learning?	No	Yes
Supports content creation?	No	Yes
Organizes reusable content?	Yes	Yes
Includes workflow tools to manage content creation?	No	Yes
Develops content navigation controls and user interface?	No	Yes

several categories of collaborative learning software, including synchronous collaboration tools and conferencing tools.

Synchronous Collaboration Tools and Live Training

Collaborative tools frequently number among synchronous WBT tools. In terms of common features and functions, synchronous web-based collaboration platforms and tools typically include shared whiteboards and chat tools. Chat tools nurture collaboration by enabling learner brainstorming and questioning, presenter clarifications and explanations, role playing, and private one-on-one mentoring. Using these tools, WLP professionals can collect immediate responses to an idea from learners around the globe. In addition, an electronic whiteboard can help learners focus on certain ideas or processes. Other common *synchronous training* tools include breakout rooms, online surveys or polling programs, file transfer programs, and discussion boards.

A key benefit of these tools includes promotion of knowledge transfer through expert demonstrations or modeling and immediate learner application. Although many complaints are associated with the stability and fidelity of video and audio elements of synchronous training, it's especially useful in sales training related to new products.

Conferencing Tools

In addition to synchronous training, opportunities exist for collaboration in asynchronous learning environments. Many conferencing tools allow learners to discuss topics at their leisure without geographical or time-zone restrictions on contributions. In fact, team meetings may take place across continents and many hours. For those who want to discuss issues in real time, conferencing tools often include synchronous chat options.

Many conferencing tools are embedded in LMSs and LCMSs. Some of these tools allow instructors to create online teams for small-group work or product development with associated drop-down menus. Many also include real-time chat tools in a discussion forum so that learners can collaborate and hold special events, such as team meetings. Feedback tools are often built in, but LMSs and LCMSs are not rich in interaction or collaboration tools because most LMS vendors assume a self-paced learner.

Learning Support Systems

Learning technologies have expanded the instructor's role to encompass far more responsibility than what's traditional for trainers (Mantyla and Gividen 1997). A traditional job description for instructors no longer exists because distance learning and the constant introduction of new technologies are creating an environment in which WLP professionals need to become more flexible and deliver training when and where the workforce needs it.

Learners want and need training, education, and information access at home, on the job, and at points in between. To provide 360-degree support, WLP professionals need to develop and maintain a systematic way of dealing with the need for information, guidance, and help in providing easy access to additional resources.

Mantyla and Gividen (1997) note several key aspects of an LSS and its required services:

- *Preparation and design of registration processes:* Current registration processes for on-site courses need to be adapted for distance learning registration. Registration options include by telephone, fax machine, mail, and electronic methods. Registration forms can capture key profile information about learners, such as job title, skill or knowledge level of the subject, desired learning outcomes, and motivation for taking the course.

- *Marketing methods and communication vehicles:* WLP professionals need to get the word out about the LSS in as many ways as possible. Based on budget and available resources, they create professional marketing pieces with the training department or a distance learning logo or branding. They identify course benefits, registration processes, contact names, quotes from enthusiastic distance learners, and a list of upcoming courses.

- *Learner-orientation tools:* These tools describe the what, where, how, who, and why of the distance learning experience. Distance learners need to know who to call with specific questions. Orientation kits for learners with the instructor's contact name; hours of availability; and addresses and numbers for mail, phone, fax, and email are helpful. To support a successful learning experience, the WLP professional should think about how to create a motivational, supportive environment from the beginning and how to encourage communication with the instructor and other learners based on learners' needs.

- *Self-directed learning resource information:* LSSs should help learners access self-directed information, whether it's about content or related readings and multimedia resources, financial guidance for taking courses, or a menu of related courses. WLP professionals should consider providing a list of references relevant to the course. Another strategy is to offer a listserv that allows learners to have a dialog with others interested in the same type of information. Recommending the listserv to learners encourages them to have a conversation by computer (known as a chat) with others, which expands networking opportunities.

Effects of Learning Information Systems

WLP professionals should be aware of the effects that the increasingly widespread use of learning information systems has and ways that learning systems may be incorporated:

- Using a learning information system can cause changes in an organization's management style and roles in the line structure by enabling it to align learning initiatives with strategic goals and offer employees courses that can enhance their career paths.

- Learning information systems promote the openness and speed of response that often accompany new technologies.

- WLP professionals may be asked to make recommendations for using an LCMS. In addition to considering an organization's business needs, WLP professionals may need to consider the cost of a learning information system, the continuing evolution of technology, challenges in customization, and interoperability with other learning material.

- Related to use of an LCMS is using an LMS to track courses and other administrative functions that may be a subset of an LCMS.

- Integration of existing systems and security issues in an organization may lead to an increased need to use information systems and deal with compatibility issues.

✓ Chapter 5 Knowledge Check

1. **Which of the following systems manages content, such as components that make up a course?**

   __ **A.** LMS

   __ **B.** LCMS

   __ **C.** LSS

   __ **D.** Collaboration tools

2. **Which of the following systems manages learners, including who's taking what, completion ratios, course progress status, and scheduling?**

   __ **A.** LMS

   __ **B.** LCMS

   __ **C.** LSS

   __ **D.** Collaboration tools

3. **Which of the following is *not* a benefit of an LCMS?**

   __ **A.** Faster development with a WYSIWYG authoring environment

   __ **B.** Collaboration and storage of learning content with check-in and check-out capabilities

   __ **C.** Reuse and the ability to create once, use many times

   __ **D.** Integration with HR systems

4. **Which of the following includes email, computer networks, whiteboards, bulletin board systems, chat rooms, and online presentation tools, which can play an important role in the expansion of e-learning and in collaborating on projects, sharing information, and communicating?**

   __ **A.** LMS

   __ **B.** LCMS

   __ **C.** LSS

   __ **D.** Collaboration tools

5. **An LMS supports pretesting and adaptive learning.**

   __ **A.** True

   __ **B.** False

6. The implementation of learning information systems can cause changes in an organization's management style and roles within the line structure.

    __ **A.** True

    __ **B.** False

---

7. An organization's training department is deciding if it should purchase a learning information system. Which of the following is *not* a likely effect of the learning information system adoption?

    __ **A.** Better able to align learning initiatives with strategic goals

    __ **B.** A need to provide LMS recommendations based on organizational needs

    __ **C.** A need to adjust to a faster speed of response

    __ **D.** Better able to deal with technology compatibility issues

---

8. Which of the following is *not* one of the assessments that should be conducted prior to implementing an LMS?

    __ **A.** IT infrastructure assessment

    __ **B.** Cultural readiness assessment

    __ **C.** Training needs assessment

    __ **D.** Administrative process analysis

---

9. A training department is collecting requirements for selecting an LCMS. Which of the following is a typical LCMS function?

    __ **A.** Manage traditional forms of training

    __ **B.** Provide learner profile management

    __ **C.** Create test questions

    __ **D.** Provide skills gap analysis functions

References

Bonk, C.J. (November 2002). "Collaborative Tools for E-Learning." *Chief Learning Officer: Solutions for Enterprise Productivity*. http://clomedia.com/articles/view /collaborative_tools_for_e_learning.

Carliner, S. (November 2005). "Course Management Systems Versus Learning Management Systems." *Learning Circuits*. www.learningcircuits.org /2005/nov2005/carliner.html.

Greenberg, L. (December 2002). "LMS and LCMS: What's the Difference?" *Learning Circuits*. (Out of print.)

Hall, S.O., and B. Hall. (November 2004). "A Guide to Learning Content Management Systems." *Training*, pp. 33–37.

Harris, P.M., and O.S. Castillo. (2002). "Instructional Design for WBT." *Infoline* No. 250202.

Mantyla, K., and J.R. Gividen. (1997). *Distance Learning: A Step-by-Step Guide for Trainers*. Alexandria, VA: ASTD Press.

Moran, J.V. (January 2002). "Mission: Buy an LMS." *Learning Circuits*. www.astd.org /LC/2002/0102_moran.htm.

6
Marketplace Resources

A major role of training managers is to determine the best approach for satisfying an organization's learning needs. Based on these needs, a training manager must be able to identify the appropriate techniques, delivery methods, and materials for each program. If in-house resources aren't available, training vendors are a key resource in delivering training or providing tools for training. Knowing the variety of vendors is necessary to provide quality training, whether it's classroom-based training; e-learning or web-based learning; or in-house training that uses reference materials, training materials, and job aids. A training manager must be able to evaluate vendors' products and services, based on the program's learning goals and objectives. This evaluation requires an understanding of the products and services available from a variety of resources.

Understanding the steps in outsourcing a training program is also an essential skill for training managers. The steps include establishing decision criteria for outsourcing; determining the budget; developing contracts and supporting documents; and identifying methods to build, monitor, and evaluate the program.

Learning Objectives:

☑ Describe one factor in selecting printed materials to support learning needs.

☑ List the marketplace resources that instructors or training managers may purchase from training vendors to meet internal training needs.

☑ Describe one consideration when selecting e-learning content from a marketplace resource.

☑ Describe one consideration when selecting web-based learning content from a marketplace resource.

☑ Discuss four factors to consider when deciding whether to use off-the-shelf versus in-house development to create training materials.

☑ Compare the advantages and disadvantages of developing materials in-house to purchasing materials from a vendor.

☑ Summarize the steps to create a request for proposal (RFP), and list two elements that are included in the RFP.

Outsourcing Training

Outsourcing training—using external resources or products to meet business needs—enables an organization to acquire specialized expertise that it doesn't want to staff full time or to provide support for in-house staff who lack certain skill sets.

This trend toward using external help is becoming the norm in light of the tremendous pressure on organizations to meet changing and sometimes unpredictable customer demands, respond to continual technology advancements, and stay one step ahead of marketplace shifts. For training managers who manage or direct the training and development function without a full staff, building a network of resources can help them succeed. Workplace learning and performance (WLP) professionals can create their own databases of vendors, categorized by expertise and abilities—whether projects are short term and narrowly focused or long term and multifaceted.

To determine each vendor's capabilities, WLP professionals can assess its products, based on qualitative and quantitative metrics; find internal customers the vendor has worked with and collect information; use a simple checklist; or conduct a quick telephone interview (asking three or four key questions). Scheduling periodic formal and informal vendor evaluations and soliciting feedback from customers at the end of every project also provides valuable information. Another important factor to consider when evaluating potential vendors is their interpersonal abilities (influencing customers, handling difficult situations, and so forth).

Vendor Assessment

To assess vendors, WLP professionals can design a quick, straightforward assessment tool or process. They should consider a variety of elements and then assign an appropriate weight to each element. The weight should depend on the organization's needs and expectations about the quality of the product or service. Elements to include in the process are

- credentials of the vendor's staff and previous experience with the vendor

- feedback from previous clients

- the degree of cohesion between the vendor's organizational philosophies and the WLP professional's organization

- the depth of the vendor's related experiences

- the vendor's staffing capabilities and quality of products.

Vendor Materials

After considering the big-picture perspective of outsourcing, WLP professionals need to evaluate the products and services that vendors provide. This process includes evaluating printed materials, training or project management services, and e-learning or web-based training materials.

Evaluating Printed Materials

Trainers do more than just lead classes and design instruction. They also must be able to train subject matter experts (SMEs) to train others and provide a variety of written materials. Trainers often need to use these materials:

- *Participant workbooks:* Used in instructor-led courses, workbooks should be designed so that participants can interact with the material, take notes, complete exercises, and capture ideas. These materials help keep learners on track by providing feedback and asking them questions within the text. Extra or remedial material and directions should be included for learners who need to backtrack. For students needing additional challenges, the workbook should provide new content or conclude with suggestion for how learners can apply instruction on the job.

- *Instructor manuals:* These often include key points to cover, what to say on a topic, times to introduce training media and activities, alternative material and strategies, training process tips, and reference and resource information.

- *Self-paced study guides:* Study guides are usually meant to be read and used from beginning to end (linear design). Emphasis may vary by subtopic, with more elaboration given to frequently used or difficult-to-grasp information.

- *Reference manuals:* These contain detailed and technical information. The best reference manuals are designed so that information is easy to find and written in clear, simple language.

- *Handouts:* Handouts are used as supplements to course material and include directions for specific exercises.

- *Job aids:* These quick visual references provide guidance or assistance, either audio or visual, to a performer about when to carry out tasks and steps, thereby reducing the amount of recall needed and minimizing error. Usually tasks that are performed with relatively low frequency, are highly complex, are likely to change in the future, or involve a high probability of error are good candidates for job aids.

When reviewing and evaluating printed materials, the training manager should consider these questions:

- Does the manual appeal to different adult learning styles by incorporating print, visuals, and hands-on activities for kinesthetic learners?

- Is the language in the manual appropriate for the intended audience—trainers, SMEs, and participants?

- Will participants be learning from materials written in their primary or secondary language? For participants unfamiliar with the language, are concrete examples and jargon-free language used in the manual?

- Are the materials free of gender, racial, age, and other bias?

- How will the materials be used (primary and secondary purposes)?

- What learning objectives should the manual help learners achieve?

- What types of materials are required as indicated from the needs analysis and current knowledge of the target population?

- Do the look and feel of the materials support the learning objectives, and are they built to last through their intended use?

- Are the manuals well written, and do they present complex information in small, consumable chunks? Are mnemonic devices, illustrations, and examples included to help make material more memorable and understandable?

- Will the material facilitate learning after training by including a table of contents, index, glossary, wide margins for note taking, and divided or color-coded sections?

Evaluating E-Learning and WBT

Many considerations are the same for evaluating e-learning and WBT materials. Off-the-shelf e-learning—including computer-based training, WBT, and other types of e-learning formats—is prepackaged training courseware that vendors develop to increase performance on skills that organizations commonly require. Organizations are drawn to this courseware because it's fairly easy to adapt or customize an e-learning package to meet organizational needs. Most organizations purchase e-learning content when they have little or no organizational resources available to develop courseware in-house.

Of course, e-learning developed for a specific organization has certain advantages:

- It includes customized content.

- It fits the organizational environment.

- It increases the internal capacity to develop e-learning content.

The less expensive option of an off-the-shelf e-learning course also has some advantages:

- Organizations get faster delivery turnaround.

- It has low staff requirements for development.

- E-learning specialists develop the courses.

Investing in e-learning courseware results in improved knowledge, skills, and attitudes (KSAs) of end users. Training departments usually have the burden of selecting and purchasing the courseware—a venture that can cost training managers their credibility if they make poor decisions. For this reason, training managers must review several e-learning courses carefully before making a purchase.

E-learning courseware is no different from any other training method. It doesn't provide a good return-on-investment (ROI) unless end users are successful at performing the learning objectives and the program achieves its overall goal of increased performance. These are several elements to consider when reviewing e-learning courseware:

- *Audience-focused text:* Effective e-learning focuses on and addresses the appropriate target population. A program for human resources managers loses its effect when the text better suits fourth graders.

- *Relevant questions:* Effective e-learning programs contain questions that stimulate thought and prompt learners to recognize the connections between the information they just learned and its application to their jobs.

- *Informative models:* Graphics that users roll their cursors over to view additional information give learners another channel for accessing information. Some learners need graphics and sound in addition to onscreen words because they retain more information when several senses are stimulated and they think they're participating actively in their learning. Good interactive learning uses models to add value and meaning, not just fill white space on a page.

- *Retrievable information:* Being able to retrieve information from a secure database is integral to interactivity. Information retrieval capability is necessary when programs ask focused questions that guide learners to input information and then take action. If participants view e-learning as a daily help tool rather than a one-time learning experience, e-learning will make huge advances in organizations. Learners could access programs to help them work through decisions on a daily basis, using a dynamic, interactive method of learning instead of the traditional static form of e-learning most people are used to.

- *Chances to collaborate:* Effective interaction in e-learning is not limited to facilitating connections between the learner and the instruction. E-learning interaction also involves connecting learners with one another. Interaction capabilities connect multiple users from anywhere in the world to participate in the same instruction and share ideas.

Off-the-Shelf, Customized, or In-House Development

If a high-quality generic course can satisfy training needs, training managers can obtain the same great ROI they would from custom-developed courses for only a fraction of the outlay, simply by securing off-the-shelf training materials. Using generic courses to improve an organization makes good business sense and can become a viable method for expanding a business team's skills.

WLP professionals need to think about how to make better buying decisions because obtaining off-the-shelf courseware has become an ongoing and essential activity for every training manager. With the increased demand created by the growth of the training audience and the speed of technical change, WLP professionals can't fulfill all training needs by developing every course from the ground up, and they can't afford to have every course to take place in a classroom environment. How does a training manager decide to buy off-the-shelf content, customize content, or develop in-house? Key factors to consider when making this decision include

- the organization's and training audience's size
- the frequency of training needed
- the proprietary nature of the training content
- sources of learning and performance products and services
- the cost for initial development or purchase and recurring costs to deliver or maintain the course
- the type of vendor price structure (for example, annual fee for all users or price-per-use fee)
- the amount and type of ongoing support
- the rate at which the content changes, requiring future updates or changes
- the experience of the vendor.

To help make the make-or-buy decision, table 6-1 summarizes the strengths and weaknesses of each solution.

Table 6-1. Developing In-House Versus Purchasing a Product

	Strengths	Weaknesses
Developing in-house	• Course designers have firsthand knowledge of the company, culture, mission, and goals. • Learning objectives can be tailored to specific needs. • Trust with internal clients and the development group is already established.	• It requires lengthy development time. • It places demands on staff to design and develop. • WLP professionals must locate the expertise required in-house. • Developing in-house assumes that in-house employees are experts.
Purchasing a product	• The product is available immediately. • The developer's expertise is available for consultation. • The product can cost less.	• Training may not meet all needs. • Time is needed to orient the contractor to the company culture. • A purchased product can't be customized. • A purchased product can be expensive.

Steps in Outsourcing

The steps in outsourcing can be thoughtfully customized to fit each organization's needs, culture, purpose, and other particular circumstances. These are the eight primary steps in the outsourcing process:

1. Determining needs

2. Defining the scope and budget

3. Creating and sending the RFP

4. Evaluating proposals and selecting a vendor

5. Notifying the vendor and negotiating the contract

6. Implementing the project

7. Monitoring the schedule

8. Completing and evaluating the project.

Step 1. Determining Needs

At the beginning of the process, decision makers need to make a commitment to selecting and carrying out the best outsourcing solution. The team that forms at this early stage, which includes the WLP professional and other stakeholders in the outsourcing project, develops a big-picture view, articulating broad project goals, taking an honest look at options, and candidly discussing hopes and fears for what using an outside vendor might mean. Based on this information, team members develop an outsourcing strategy. When assessing the goals and needs for outsourcing, the WLP professional should identify

- market trends and competitive position

- goals and objectives (improve quality, reduce costs, and so forth)

- baseline costs and metrics (labor, infrastructure, and vendor costs) compared with benchmarks

- opportunities for restructuring and design

- model cash flows for each option

- benefits and risks for each option

- required competencies to ensure that the organization has enough resources.

Step 2. Defining the Scope and Budget

In this step, the outsourcing team details what they outlined in the determining needs step and in the commitment to move forward with outsourcing. Activities include identifying functions or tasks, analyzing outsourcing options, and making a preliminary choice about which ones (if any) are the most likely candidates for outsourcing. In this step, the team identifies the full range of sourcing options—internal, contractual, and consulting—for each activity and develops a budget. The list of potential activities to be considered for outsourcing varies by situation.

The team develops a pool of potential suppliers and criteria for measuring each one. By undertaking rigorous analysis based on the organization's needs and vendors' expertise, an organization (and its prospective vendors) can make a sound decision about *whether*, on *what*, and *how best* to work together. Not only does this step result in selecting vendors, but it also yields critical information to begin shaping a contract.

To identify potential vendors and criteria for assessing vendors, the team needs to identify the business criteria and goals, as outlined in the business case, and then apply the criteria uniformly to all vendors for a fair and accurate assessment and weight the criteria to reflect the priorities. A grid such as the one in table 6-2 can be a useful tool in clarifying and prioritizing criteria and ensuring that vendors are assessed uniformly.

These broad criteria are likely to be on the list for consideration: cost, quality, capabilities, customer service, stability, experience, shared values, and cultural fit. Most are standard for measuring potential vendors, even for contracted services. They should not be the only measures, particularly if the desired outcome is an arrangement more like a partnership than the typical supplier–customer model. Therefore, the team must select criteria according to how well they reinforce the overall purpose.

Step 3. Creating and Sending the RFP

Having defined and identified its needs, an organization uses an RFP to communicate its requirements to potential vendors and define how those requirements are measured. An RFP introduces the organization, its background and goals, its culture and values, and

Table 6-2. Comparison of Vendors

Criteria	Weight	Vendor A	Vendor B	Vendor C
Cost				
Quality				
Capabilities				
Customer service				
Stability				
Experience				
Shared values				
Cultural fit				
Other (distance learning capability, industry expertise, past experience)				

its specific needs. This document also asks for parallel information from the vendor. In particular, an RFP asks the vendor to explain its capabilities for supplying the needed services, at what cost, and at what level of quality. An RFP reflects the criteria the team has developed and notes ways to assess how each prospective supplier measures up in each area.

RFPs include these elements:

- *executive summary:* a synopsis of the vendor's product or service
- *company information:* information about the vendor's company size, structure, experience, and expertise
- *deliverables:* an outline of how the vendor will meet the customer's needs
- *references:* a list of previous vendor customers
- *outlined development process:* a detailed description of the plan, objectives, scope of effort, and timeline
- *cost:* details about how the vendor will charge for services (for example, training cost per day, travel and entertainment expenses extra, content development hourly or daily rates, and project management fees).

When the team has completed—or nearly completed—defining its selection criteria, team members can begin the search for potential providers.

Step 4. Evaluating Proposals and Selecting a Vendor

When an organization receives proposals back from vendors, having discussions—often in the form of presentations—in which the company and prospective vendor explore in more depth how they would work together is important. The team needs to find out what has worked well, what has not, how progress has been made, and how problems have been solved in the past. Probing areas that are significant for the company and recognizing where differences between cultures may lead to appropriately different structures and systems is also important. The RFP and follow-up conversations should make it possible for the team to compare prospective suppliers with quantitative information and to gain a deeper qualitative understanding of each vendor.

For the list of criteria to be useful, the team needs a system of analysis that enables comparing each potential vendor with the others. Charles H. Kepner and Benjamin B. Tregoe (1981) describe a practical, straightforward decision-making process. First, they divide criteria into musts and wants. The musts are defined in either/or categories. For example, one must is for vendors to have technical support sufficient to handle 120,000 registrations per month. The first round of analysis measures vendors against this criterion: Do they have this capacity or not? Those that don't are no longer considered.

The wants are relative measures that are important but can't be quantified into yes-or-no answers. In the registration technology example, the organization wants to increase the quantity of training and education it offers, so it's looking for a supplier with a strong commitment to leading-edge technology that would enable it to keep pace with the organization's projected growth. In this case, the organization would look for a vendor that shows this commitment *more than the others*. In this situation, the team's assessment is qualitative rather than binary. The question becomes "Who is the best?"

This situation is where a weighted comparison of suppliers can be useful (see table 6-3). This tool provides a structure for identifying wants that have the highest value and for weighting them accordingly. By giving careful consideration to weights in relation to the organization's goals for outsourcing, the team arrives at a numeric reflection of how well each vendor meets the outsourcing goals instead of an objective but perhaps irrelevant evaluation of these vendors.

As shown in table 6-3, the next steps are to create a weighted analysis of the company's wants. The vendors that make it to this cut have already passed the must screening. This tool helps force healthy discussion about priorities and understanding how well each vendor may be able to meet them.

Step 5. Notifying the Vendor and Negotiating the Contract

A contract is a necessary document that forms the legal agreement between an organization and its outsourcing supplier. It establishes guidelines for working together and addresses a number of specific issues. It also spells out a way for the organization to part ways if things don't work out.

The two contracting parties are partners and allies in delivering services and seeking to win customer satisfaction, but the supplier wants to maximize profits, and the customer wants to minimize costs. The supplier wants to minimize risks or commitments; the customer wants to maximize the promise of reliable performance. The hope is that the contract holds these elements in creative tension to the benefit of both parties, but it can do so only if it's seen as a reflection of work already done by both parties and their intentions for the future of their relationship. Typically, this doesn't happen if the contracting process is handed off to the legal or financial department in isolation from the team.

Table 6-3. Weighted Comparison of Suppliers

Want Criterion	Priority Weight	Supplier A Score	Wt.	Supplier B Score	Wt.	Supplier C Score	Wt.
Distance learning capability	10	8	80	7	70	10	100
Industry experience	9	10	90	9	81	9	81
Implementation in six months	8	10	80	7	56	8	64
Totals			250		207		245

Nearly as many different approaches to contracting exist as do organizations. Some examples include these:

- *Firm fixed price:* The product or service is clearly defined (for example, a presentation, video, or generic program).

- *Cost plus fixed price:* Analysis and development are involved, and a negotiated percentage of the overall cost is identified as profit. Government procurement offices often use this procedure.

- *Cost plus incentive fee:* When time is critical, the resource gets a bonus if the contract is completed ahead of schedule. The reverse is also possible, in which the contract imposes a penalty for missed deadlines.

- *Performance based:* A certain percentage of the fixed fee is based on employees' successful performance on the job. This approach works only when desired performance can be described and measured specifically.

Regardless of the type of contract, organizations and their suppliers need to create a contract that's a brief, written expression of an understanding between two parties. The contract serves as a platform for a lasting architecture, balances the needs of organizations and suppliers, and paves the way for future success. Activities in preparing a contract include setting goals and performance measures, deciding what to negotiate, and determining the process for changing requirements.

Before entering into contract negotiations, the outsourcing team needs to benchmark the systems it proposes to outsource and establish baseline measures of performance. What's written into the contract should be an expression of the homework already done—the goals both parties agree to, based on appropriate measures and realistic baseline data. Other information negotiated at this point should include data or reproduction rights, penalties, payment schedules, a fee structure, and a schedule of deliveries.

To ensure that the vendor meets the organization's needs, regular feedback should be documented in the contract. A vendor not improving a product or service after specific feedback, as indicated in the contract, constitutes a breach of contract and reason to cancel it. The contract should be specific about quality, quantity, and deadlines.

Another specific item for parties to negotiate is the length of the contract period. A three- to four-year contract, with the option for rolling renewals, often works best. At the end of each year, the contract is renegotiated for the next three years. Within a longer-term framework, however, a six-month review is needed, along with an escape clause. If the relationship isn't working and is clearly not going to work, both parties should agree to dissolve the partnership as soon as possible. The first six months is, therefore, viewed as a trial period.

When appropriate, the outsourcing team might want to consider a sliding-fee scale for varying levels of experience and expertise in the vendor's staff. Organizations should be wary of vendors that use the organization as a training ground for their new consultants. Typically, this is more of an issue on long-term projects with multiple components. Managing who is doing what on these projects can be difficult. For this reason, establishing specific quality checkpoints and scheduled performance feedback is critical. The outsourcing team needs to establish criteria for success before hiring the vendor.

Nearly every outsourcing arrangement is subject to the same dilemma: In the beginning, the organization decides to outsource six items, but even before the ink on the contract is dry, it becomes clear that adding two or three more items to the list makes sense. When the relationship works well, that will probably continue to happen. Contracts always involve a trade-off: The tighter the contract, the less flexibility but also the less trouble in getting immediate requirements met. Still, many outsourcing arrangements have difficulties with long-term contracts, particularly those that are heavily linked to technology. A contract should spell out how to deal with contract changes.

Step 6. Implementing the Project

After the outsourcing team has made decisions about vendors and outlined key expectations in the contract, the next step is to complete a plan for moving activities incrementally to vendors. A project plan helps guide the transition, and milestones indicate goals for measuring progress at regular intervals.

Generally, transitions are smoother when they take the form of complete processes that include periodic feedback and adjustment. Formalizing a plan for the transition reaps benefits not only in moving the process forward, but also in creating a calm atmosphere. The plan becomes a reality when people oversee, manage, and communicate it.

Step 7. Monitoring the Schedule

As part of the schedule, the outsourcing team should identify, define, and include several milestones in the project plan. These milestones may serve as points of evaluation and decisions and often correlate with measures of success. One way of determining milestones is to review measures of success and use them as a logical framework. For example, the first phase of the transition might be to migrate the first set of courses to the vendor. Before this phase starts, the team establishes goals and measures of success, gaining agreement with the vendor. Completing the first set of courses and collecting data from them is a logical place to review performance against goals and measures. It's a natural point at which to set a milestone on the project plan.

At regular intervals, as indicated with milestones, or perhaps at weekly or monthly status meetings or conference calls, the outsourcing team and vendors should discuss progress compared with the baseline milestones outlined in the project plan. Evaluating the quality of the vendor's outputs as the work unfolds adds depth to the relationship between the outsourcing team and the vendor. In essence, giving feedback on the product quality or methods helps manage expectations and deadlines. The contract should include a process for periodic feedback. For long-term projects, this process is especially important.

Feedback should focus on performance and be based on the criteria established for success. If something happens that affects production, quality, or interpersonal relationships, the outsourcing team should give feedback immediately (or as close to the time of the event as possible). The feedback mechanism can be as simple as a checklist of productivity and quality criteria. Thinking about the appropriate mechanism and criteria ahead of time helps avoid spending money on something the outsourcing team doesn't want or expect.

Step 8. Completing and Evaluating the Project

Just as the team managed the project according to goals and milestones set out in the project plan, periodic reviews should have captured best practices and items requiring improvement. All those best practices and all that historical information should be kept in some sort of project repository, such as file cabinets, electronic documentation on a **server**, or a database. These best practices and lessons learned prevent the team from having to reinvent the wheel later by documenting processes, quality checklists, and so on that should continue to be leveraged.

Just as a project plan must be in place for the transition of processes to a vendor, a transition plan should be in place in case any ongoing functions need to move back in-house. The outsourcing team may need to plan to train internal staff on systems, functions, or processes the vendor previously handled that will now be the organization's ongoing responsibility.

✓ Chapter 6 Knowledge Check

1. **Before making a decision to purchase printed participant materials, the training director always insists on checking if a table of contents, an index, and a glossary are included. Why is checking these components important when reviewing printed training materials?**

   __ **A.** Determines the overall quality of the materials

   ↘ **B.** Facilitates learning after training

   __ **C.** Prepares the instructor for class

   __ **D.** Appeals to different adult learning styles

2. **All of the following are key elements to consider when reviewing off-the-shelf e-learning courseware** *except*

   __ **A.** Audience-focused text

   __ **B.** Informative models

   ↘ **C.** Revision schedules

   __ **D.** Chances to collaborate

3. **Many considerations are different when evaluating e-learning versus web-based training materials.**

   __ **A.** True

   ↘ **B.** False

4. **Outsourcing usually refers to deciding whether to use external products and resources to meet business needs.**

   ↘ **A.** True

   __ **B.** False

5. **An organization needs to develop a training program to support a new product launch and salesforce training. Which of the following is the best benefit of developing materials and training programs in-house?**

   __ **A.** The end product may have a lower cost because in-house expertise is used.

   ↘ **B.** Designers and developers have firsthand knowledge of the company, culture, mission, and goals.

   __ **C.** Development time is shorter.

   __ **D.** All resources are available immediately.

6. **A key benefit of outsourcing includes identifying how to best use internal resources and leverage external resources.**

   ↘ **A.** True

   ✗ **B.** False

7. **Of the following, who developed a decision-making model for comparing potential vendors by dividing criteria into musts and wants and applying weightings to those items?**

   __ **A.** Kepner-Tregoe

   __ **B.** Gardner

   __ **C.** Herrmann

   __ **D.** Knowles

---

8. **Which of the following best describes a firm fixed-price contract?**

   __ **A.** The product or service can be clearly defined (for example, a presentation, video, or generic program).

   __ **B.** Analysis and development are involved, and a negotiated percentage of the overall cost is identified as profit. Government procurement offices often use this procedure.

   __ **C.** When time is critical, the resource gets a bonus if the contract is completed ahead of schedule. The reverse is also possible, in which the contract imposes a penalty for missed deadlines.

   __ **D.** A certain percentage of the fixed fee is added based on employees' successful performance on the job. This works only when desired performance can be described and measured specifically.

---

9. **All the following are standard elements of an RFP *except***

   __ **A.** Development process and timeline

   __ **B.** Deliverables

   __ **C.** References

   __ **D.** Financial statements

---

10. **Which of the following is *not* a main step in the outsourcing process?**

   __ **A.** Determining needs, scope, and budget

   __ **B.** Creating the RFP

   __ **C.** Contract negotiation

   __ **D.** Conducting trainer interviews

11. **Which of the following types of contracts requires analysis and development and also has a negotiated percentage of the overall cost identified as profit?**

    __ **A.** Firm fixed price

    __ **B.** Cost plus fixed price

    __ **C.** Cost plus incentive fee

    __ **D.** Performance based

References

Cowan, S.L. (2000). "Outsourcing Training." *Infoline* No. 250002.

Dearden, J. (1999). "Evaluating Off-the-Shelf CBT Courseware." *Infoline* No. 259908.

DeRose, G.J. (1999). *Outsourcing Training and Education.* Alexandria, VA: ASTD Press.

Francis, L. (September 2001). "Expect More From E-Learning." *Learning Circuits.* www .learningcircuits.org/2001/sep2001/elearn.html.

Kepner, C.H., and B.B. Tregoe. (1981). *The New Rational Manager.* Princeton, NJ: Princeton Research Press.

Nilson, C. (1999). *How to Start a Training Program.* Alexandria, VA: ASTD Press.

Novak, C. (1997). "High Performance Training Manuals." *Infoline* No. 259707. (Out of print.)

Piskurich, G.M., P. Beckschi, and B. Hall, editors. (2000). *The ASTD Handbook of Training Design and Delivery.* New York: McGraw-Hill.

Sandler, S.F., editor. (May 2004). "Planning to Outsource." *HRFocus,* pp. 1–15.

7
Understanding Program Administration

Learning, development, and performance programs should relate closely to the strategy of the workplace learning and performance (WLP) professional's organization and be part of a training policy that demonstrates the value of learning to the organization. To demonstrate return-on-investment (ROI), WLP professionals must build measurement into learning and performance programs and develop and institute a means to communicate value so that they can justify and obtain program funding.

Learning Objectives:

☑ Define program administration.

☑ List six responsibilities in the role of a training manager.

☑ Describe the purpose of the following components of a program curriculum: topics, outlines, objectives, courseware, media, and delivery methods.

☑ State two considerations of managing facility equipment and resources.

☑ Describe two considerations for assigning instructors to train specific courses.

☑ Discuss considerations for using subject matter experts (SMEs) to provide training.

Program Administration

The learning function in an organization is responsible for all aspects of identifying learning and performance needs and designing, developing, and delivering or procuring the required solutions to meet an organization's needs. The training manager is primarily responsible for identifying needs, developing a strategy to meet target learners' needs, and securing resources to fill those needs. Program administration, another aspect of a training manager's role, includes factors such as managing program elements to support the delivery of training; securing equipment and resources; identifying and training instructors; managing logistics, including course registration, scheduling, and locations; and working with SMEs as needed.

The Role of the Training Manager

The training manager is the person in the organization responsible for all training projects and delivery. The role of a training manager includes

- ensuring that programs support the organization's goals and vision
- gaining leadership's support to ensure that employees attend and participate in learning initiatives
- planning and budgeting for programs
- staffing and delivering programs
- monitoring and maintaining quality of delivery and services
- demonstrating ROI for programs—in essence, closing the loop and demonstrating the learning function's value to supporting company goals and objectives.

Program Elements

Several core elements define and support the development and delivery of learning and performance programs. Table 7-1 describes some of the most common elements.

The training manager is responsible for ensuring that program elements support the learning objectives, but another responsibility that should not be taken lightly is evaluating training. Training evaluation should not be based solely on whether learners liked the course, but on whether they are able to meet the training objectives when they walk out of the classroom—and, most important, when they are back on the job.

Trainers

Successful trainers share a number of characteristics. First, they must have a thorough, comprehensive knowledge of the subject they are teaching. Material should be presented clearly and straightforwardly, using language and written materials geared to learners' comprehension level. Competent trainers demonstrate a sincere concern for and interest in learners' progress and well-being. They also show an interest in finding out more about learners' abilities and encouraging them to strengthen and develop their strong points.

Table 7-1. Common Elements of Learning Programs

Element	Description
Program curriculum	Big-picture perspective of what types of courses and content the training organization offers, for example, customer service training, new hire training, and sales representative training.
Topics	Within a curriculum, a list of topics is derived from the results of analysis. The topics relate to the knowledge and skills an employee needs to meet the baseline KSAs for a job. Topics are often classified into need-to-know and nice-to-know content.
Outlines	Based on the list of topics and types of skills that need to be trained (for example, cognitive or psychomotor), course designers develop course outlines during the analysis or design phases. These outlines may include some initial self-study content, such as reading material, to give target learners background information and level their baseline knowledge. Other course outlines may include instructor-led or other technology-delivered training for all content in the curriculum.
Objectives	As part of the design process, after course designers develop a course outline that organizes topics and types of skills needed, they develop training objectives in the A-B-C-D format—defining each element of an objective, including audience, behavior, condition, and degree.
Courseware	After the designer develops course objectives, courseware and evaluation content development can begin. Courseware may include self-study guides, job aids, instructor-led materials, technology-delivered training deliverables, and assessments.
Media	Media, also referred to as presentation methods, refers to the types of technology used to present training content, including audio, video, computer-based training (CBT), electronic text, electronic performance support system, multimedia, online help, and teleconferencing.
Delivery methods	A number of delivery methods used for training include • instructor-led or classroom training, which usually involves one or more learners with a facilitator in a single location who may or may not use an overhead projector, a slide projector, a laptop computer, or a flipchart and easel

Delivery methods, continuted	• technology-facilitated training, often referred to as multimedia, CBT, e-learning, virtual reality, and so forth, which uses technology to deliver learning to learners in a single location and may or may not include a live facilitator • distance learning (for example, teleconferencing), which involves learners at one or more different physical locations than the source of the instruction • on-the-job training • distributed learning, which may include home study courses where training is distributed by a process, such as mail, that's not related to implementation • learning technologies, which may be synchronous or asynchronous.

To help learners progress and overcome problems, effective trainers work on a one-to-one basis with students. In addition to providing practical applications for training, instructors can show them how to use their new knowledge or skills on the job. Last, top-notch trainers should be comfortable enough to approach the learning environment with a sense of humor, using laughter to lighten rather than create tension.

When looking for trainers, consider these:

- Confirm what skills or knowledge learners need to perform their jobs successfully. This information may be available from comprehensive needs or task analyses. The profile of target learners and learning objectives of the instruction also help in determining which trainers are most appropriate to conduct the training.

- Identify trainers with information and solid background in the content to be trained. Learners can spot an ill-prepared trainer in a flash. Trainers who are poorly prepared may have to spend the rest of the course trying to recover learners' cooperation and confidence. The WLP professional should set ground rules about expectations for the amount of preparation and depth of knowledge he or she expects trainers to have before conducting the course.

- Trainers show their commitment to their work, profession, or field, and their enthusiasm for training the course materials through their gestures and activity. The best way to motivate learners is to have a trainer who is truly motivated as well.

- Trainers demonstrating concern for and interest in learners help build safe learning environments, in which learners actively participate. By showing these qualities, instructors demonstrate that they understand and at times share learners' points of view and present them in an objective and articulate fashion.

- Trainers need to maintain flexibility about both subject matter and participants. They should be open and adaptable when conceptualizing topics and themes for the instruction and should always be willing to listen and learn from the group.

Facilities: Equipment and Resources

Two key assets for training delivery that must be planned, coordinated, and managed are equipment and resources. Before training managers begin the facility selection process, they need to know the program's learning objectives and then plan for a physical setting that supports those objectives. Because presentation techniques must be adapted to the ways adults learn, training managers should account for them in selecting facilities.

Most rooms in which training takes place accommodate a wide range of uses. They can serve as movie theaters, storage rooms, classrooms, and even restaurants. Given the inevitable limitations of a multipurpose space, training managers should strive to adapt the facility for learning as well as possible. Chairs must make people comfortable (but not too comfortable), and tables must be movable yet stable. Restrooms must be available for use by a large number of people in a short period of time and must be wheelchair accessible.

In addition, a way to check the adequacy of room dimensions is to judge all distances based on the width of the screen used for visual presentations. These are some guidelines:

- The distance from the screen to the last row of seats should not exceed six screen widths.

- The distance from the screen to the front row of seats should be at least twice the width of the screen. Participants who are closer than that may experience discomfort and fatigue.

- The proper width of the viewing area is three screen widths. No one should sit more than one screen width to the left or right of the screen.

- The room's ceiling should be high enough—a minimum of nine feet—to permit people seated in the last row to see the bottom of the screen over, not around, the heads of those in front of them.

- If possible, screens should recede into the ceiling and raise and lower automatically.

For more information, see Module 2, *Delivering Training,* chapter 4, "Training Delivery Options and Media."

Subject Matter Experts

SMEs often work with training managers and learning design team members to help with various aspects of designing or delivering training. SMEs fall into one of two general categories: Some have expertise in a specific skill, and others have more conceptual or knowledge-based expertise.

SMEs are often asked to provide a combination of services. Asking an SME to teach an already designed program requires the least work for an SME. Requiring an SME to assist an instructional designer in curriculum creation allows the SME to work with an instructional design expert. In this situation, the SME and instructional designer create the program with the designer, using the SME's knowledge to develop a curriculum.

Often an SME is asked to take the lead in designing and developing a program. This can lead to failure because the SME is not an instructional designer. In this case, a training manager needs to work with SMEs to ensure that they understand the steps in this process.

Selecting an SME to Train

In today's environment of using fewer dollars to conduct top-notch training, using SMEs to train makes economic sense. For some topics, it could take training generalists weeks, if not months, to get up to speed enough on a technical process or a job skill to prepare a curriculum. Training managers don't always have the luxury of selecting an SME to conduct instruction, but when given the option, they should consider these:

- *Subject matter expertise:* An SME trainer needs to have a thorough, comprehensive knowledge of the subject to be trained. This means having the skills, knowledge, and ability to meet the minimum standard for conducting the designed training program. Ideally, an SME trainer exceeds these standards. Although having an instructional designer design and develop the curriculum is preferable, the reality is that SMEs are often asked to design and deliver training. When SMEs need to be responsible for both training design and delivery, ensuring that they exceed the minimum standard is essential.

- *Communication skills:* A good SME trainer must be able to communicate with learners. Communication skills can be divided into two categories: presence and relationships. First, SMEs must have a confident and inviting presence and be comfortable in front of a group or in a one-on-one situation. Relationships define how people establish rapport and interact with others. To be an effective trainer, an SME must be empathetic and sympathetic yet confident, knowledgeable, and forceful enough to teach skills, behavior, and information.

- *Adult learning principles:* SMEs should have some foundational knowledge about adult learning principles and characteristics of adult learning. Applying these principles to the training environment is a different skill set and comes with experience. SMEs should be aware of how adult learning principles, styles, and characteristics affect the transfer of learning.

- *Desire:* WLP professionals should not select SMEs who don't want to be involved in the transfer of learning. Reluctant trainers make bad trainers; and no one will gain from the experience. To aid learning transfer, SMEs should be enthusiastic about their jobs and want to impart their knowledge to others.

Preparing an SME to Train

After an SME has been assigned to deliver training, a training manager should take inventory of the SME's skills and qualifications compared with the program's learning objectives. Training managers may need to ask SMEs to deliver instruction from already existing content or to develop and deliver the content. When working with SMEs to deliver instruction, training managers should consider these:

- *The learning outcome:* This is the most basic element an SME must understand. Training managers must give clear parameters for results of the instruction. For example, at the end of the instruction, participants will be able to demonstrate all of the steps required to make widget Y on the assembly line.

- *The learning audience:* Any trainer, SME or not, needs to know the defining qualities of participants. At a minimum, the SME should know the group's composition, comfort level in learning from a computer screen or print materials, and prerequisite knowledge and ensure that the material allows for flexible learning styles.

- *Methods of delivery:* Because training may be delivered using a variety of instructional methods and media, training managers need to ensure that SMEs are comfortable with both the instructional methods and the media used to deliver the training.

Preparing an SME to Work on Course Design and Development

When selecting SMEs to work on course design and development, training managers should consider them primarily for their subject matter expertise, not their instructional design capability. Training managers need to ensure that SMEs understand the basics of creating an effective instructional program, including

- conducting a needs analysis to determine training requirements
- designing the training program
- developing instructional materials and testing the program
- delivering or implementing the program
- evaluating the effectiveness of the training program.

For more information, see Module 1, *Designing Learning,* chapter 6, "Content Knowledge From SMEs."

✓ Chapter 7 Knowledge Check

1. A training director is developing a job description for a program administrator. Which of the following tasks best represents a program administrator's role?

___ A. Identifying learning and performance needs

___ B. Designing training

___ C. Developing a strategy to meet learners' needs

___ D. Managing program elements to support training delivery

2. A manager of the learning function has been informed that budget cuts of 50 percent are being instituted across the organization. What programs should be cut?

___ A. The programs currently conducted by an external vendor

___ B. The most expensive programs to administer and maintain

___ C. All instructor-led training because distance learning is less expensive

___ D. The programs that aren't strategically aligned with the organization's goals and vision

3. A training manager is working on assigning trainers to courses for the next quarter. When making these staffing assignments, the primary considerations include all the following *except*

___ A. Trainer's knowledge of the subject matter

___ B. Trainer's ability to adhere firmly to the course outline

___ C. Trainer's ability to demonstrate enthusiasm and interest in learners

___ D. Current knowledge and skill level of target learners

4. A training manager's responsibilities include all the following *except*

___ A. Staffing programs

___ B. Planning and budgeting for training programs

___ C. Ensuring that instructional programs support the organization's goals and objectives

___ D. Developing multimedia content to include in instruction

5. The learning objectives of instruction affect planning and selecting a facility.

___ A. True

___ B. False

6. **A training director is developing a big-picture perspective of the types of courses and content the organization offers. What is this director developing?**

    __ **A.** Course outline

    __ **B.** Learning objectives

    ✓ **C.** Program curriculum

    __ **D.** Topics

7. **Which of the following should *not* be a consideration when selecting an instructor?**

    ✓ **A.** Knowledge of the LMS and how to navigate

    __ **B.** Motivation level of the trainees

    __ **C.** Enthusiasm for the content being taught

    __ **D.** Relationships that the instructor has within the trainee population

8. **SMEs are usually a project's primary content resource and have deep knowledge of designing and writing training materials.**

    __ **A.** True

    ✓ **B.** False

9. **When selecting an SME to help develop training, which of the following is an essential prerequisite?**

    __ **A.** A strong background in adult learning

    ✓ **B.** Enthusiastic about his or her job

    __ **C.** Ability to discuss and train on other facets of the business

    __ **D.** Strong skills in using the LCMS

References

Carliner, S. (2003). *Training Design Basics*. Alexandria, VA: ASTD Press.

Finkel, C., and A.D. Finkel. (2000). "Facilities Planning." *Infoline* No. 258504.

Goldsmith, J.J. (2000). "Development Teams for Creating Technology-Based Training." *The ASTD Handbook of Training Design and Delivery*, G.M. Piskurich, P. Beckschi, and B. Hall, editors. New York: McGraw-Hill.

Hodell, C. (2000). *ISD From the Ground Up*. Alexandria, VA: ASTD Press.

Russo, C.S. (1999). "Teaching SMEs to Train." *Infoline* No. 259911.

Sanders, E.S. (1999). "Learning Technologies." *Infoline* No. 259902.

Seagraves, T. (2004). *Quick! Show Me Your Value*. Alexandria, VA: ASTD Press.

Sharpe, C. (1997). "How to Create a Good Learning Environment." *Infoline* No. 258506.

8
Budgeting, Accounting, and Financial Management

Strategic planning can be described as formulating, developing, implementing, and evaluating how the organization will reach its objectives. A training manager should be prepared to work with management at an organizational decision-making level and to define the training department's role within the corporate strategic plan. This process involves the major business units, including information technology, human resources (HR) and training, finance and accounting, sales and marketing, and operations.

An organization's mission, vision, and values determine how much of its budget is dedicated to training employees. Some organizations may dedicate 2 percent of the budget to training; others may dedicate 20 percent. No percentage is the right one. It depends on the organization's needs, the ability of the training department to meet those needs, and the organization's ability to get employees to training sessions.

Learning and performance solutions are most effective when they're part of an interconnected system of workplace policies and procedures designed to improve performance. If training activities are independent of other organizational systems, employees tend to question whether training matters. For example, an obvious sign of a disconnect between training and other organizational systems is training departments failing to use performance reviews to determine specific training needs or to make employees accountable for developing in areas identified as opportunities for improvement. Performance data clearly indicates organizational or individual needs, and if learning and performance solutions don't address these needs, the organization will perceive the training department as weak, with little accountability.

However, when the training department constructs training offerings and budgets based on performance data for current and future needs, accountability is tremendous. Workplace learning and performance (WLP) professionals become responsible for plugging gaps, and organizations realize that cutting training budgets has a direct effect on organizational performance.

Learning Objectives:

- ☑ Discuss the four-phased process for developing a strategic plan.
- ☑ Explain the role of the training manager in the strategic planning process.
- ☑ Define the following accounting terms: *assets, liabilities, equity, balance sheet,* and *income statement.*
- ☑ Define *budget management,* and list five budget expenses training managers plan for and manage during this process.

Strategic Plan Development

WLP professionals should link training not only to existing programs and systems, but also to current and future business needs. Organizational priorities should be the focus of the training function. However, WLP professionals should think beyond organizational priorities, using their knowledge of workplace, workforce, and population trends to demonstrate the connection between business strategy and employee development and to determine the focus of the department.

Beyond linking training to business strategy, training can be used as a business strategy in and of itself. For example, if an organization has a high turnover rate in a specific department or area, perhaps a higher investment in training for these areas or a different type of training could lower employee turnover levels.

Strategic planning can be defined as the process of systematically organizing the future, a process in which managers and other professionals use past experience as a filter for future decisions. This working definition helps focus attention on the real meaning of strategic planning. Strategic planning focuses attention on desired department outcomes and should address these questions:

- Where is the department now?
- Where does the department want to go?
- How will the department get there?
- What are the department's strengths and weaknesses?

WLP departments can develop strategic plans by using the four-phase process shown in table 8-1. Strategic planning is as much a philosophy as a plan. Training managers should use strategic planning as a tool to accomplish more things that are critical to the training function and to the overall business strategy. For that reason, strategic planning should not be a one-time event; it should be an ongoing process.

Phase 1. Formulation

Strategic planning begins with identifying organizational values and mission, vision, and value statements. Organizational culture defines expectations about behavior and about how work is done, how decisions are made, and how people communicate.

Developing a Mission

Defining the training department's mission provides a sense of purpose and direction. WLP professionals should compare the mission with the organization's overall mission statement to ensure that it reflects the organization's direction.

A mission statement focuses WLP professionals on a common outcome. It can guide training managers in making decisions and focusing the training function's role within the organization. In addition, it communicates the types of solutions and strategies the training department uses to improve the organization's effectiveness, profitability, and

Table 8-1. Four Phases of Strategic Plan Development

Phase	Tasks
1. Formulation	• Identify organizational values. • Develop mission, vision, and value statements.
2. Development	• Conduct an analysis of strengths, weaknesses, opportunities, and threats (SWOT). • Establish strategic goals (two to three years to attain). • Develop strategies to attain those goals.
3. Implementation	• Establish short-term objectives (six months to a year). • Create action plans to reach those objectives. • Allocate resources to work toward those objectives. • Motivate employees to reach those objectives.
4. Evaluation	• Review strategies. • Measure performance. • Take corrective action.

competitiveness. Therefore, the mission statement should serve as a guide to developing objectives for the training function.

Developing a Vision

In the realm of organizational planning, developing a vision begins with the future, not the present. It focuses on the end state, not on the means of getting there. The description of that exciting, ideal end state is called a *vision*.

A vision describes an organization as its members would like it to be, in terms of corporate image, values, employee satisfaction, markets, and products or services. The vision focuses on organizational strengths and uniqueness. A vision is flexible; it can adapt to changing ideas, technology, and circumstances. This also applies to developing a vision for the WLP department.

Does the training department really need a vision? A vision helps guide, remind, inspire, and control. A vision guides a training department by aligning its work with the organization's overall goals and priorities, and it can keep the department focused on what it does best and away from unrelated activities. Finally, a vision enables the training function to leave the past behind and move into a fresh future.

According to consultant Mark Graham Brown (Younger 1991), one of the keys to a successful vision is the vision statement. To keep a vision statement from becoming a useless slogan, Brown suggests that it be

- brief so that WLP employees can remember it without having to look at a wallet card or a poster

- verifiable so that people can agree on whether they have achieved it

- focused on major goals or on one or two elements of performance critical to the department's success

- understandable to all to communicate clear direction to WLP employees so that they can help the department get there

- inspirational to make WLP employees feel good about their department's direction and motivate them to help achieve the vision.

Creating Value Statements

Value statements are specific descriptions of the value the WLP professional or learning function has brought or is proposing to bring to the organization in terms of how much performance improvement the learning function has enabled, how much financial gain the performance improvement has created, why sharing this information is relevant, and what the learning function needs so that it can create even more value in the future.

Value statements are stated in a concise format that enables WLP professionals to communicate value in 30 seconds or less:

- The first segment addresses performance value, which introduces the learning department's work and describes how much value the learning department has added or plans to add in performance terms.

- The second segment describes the financial or business value. Here the WLP professional translates what performance improvement means in terms of financial measures or business metrics that the people, usually executives in the organization, care about most.

- The third segment is the relevant context, where the WLP professional connects the financial or business value with an urgent or important task the audience is dealing with currently.

- The final section is the learning function's goal. Goals are important to include in communication for several reasons, one of which is that the audience needs to know what to provide to help the learning function continue to create value. The goal statement supplies key pieces of information about sustainability and speed and helps build WLP professionals' confidence and influence.

The following example combines all these components:

Six months after implementing the stress management program, nursing turnover decreased by 20 percent. This result helped increase the organization's operating profit margin and free cash by saving $250,000 in out-of-pocket costs. This means the training department has the ability to continue funding salaries for several general administrative staff members in next year's budget. Although times are tight, the organization needs to keep all of its staff to produce these kinds of results again next year. In the next two days,

I would like to meet with you to review a proposal for how to get the CFO to increase next year's budget allocations for WLP.

Phases 2 and 3. Development and Implementation

The next step in developing a strategic plan includes creating a SWOT analysis, also known as an internal and external environmental analysis. This analysis helps WLP professionals determine their strengths and weaknesses (internal) and their opportunities and threats (external). Another purpose of this analysis is to identify the contingencies that aid and prevent achieving the department's mission. From this analysis, the training manager should make adjustments to compensate for constraints and weaknesses and build on opportunities and strengths.

WLP professionals should consider two types of environmental analysis:

1. *Internal:* Internal environmental analysis considers the organization's financial condition, managerial abilities and attitudes, facilities, staffing size and quality, competitive position, image, and structure.

2. *External:* External environmental analysis considers such elements as the organization's economic condition, legal and political realities, social and cultural values, the state of technology, the availability of resources, and the organization's competitive structure.

Strategic Goals

After identifying the training department's values, developing the mission statement and vision, and conducting the SWOT analysis, the training manager should develop strategic goals and objectives. The mission statement suggests where the program is coming from; goals and objectives indicate where it will go. These goals and objectives make up the substructure of the strategic plan.

The purpose of each goal and objective should be to accomplish the broader mission of the training program. WLP professionals who fail to filter their goals and objectives through the training function's mission will find themselves off course and awaken to the realization that they are engaged in activities they weren't intending or qualified to accomplish.

Some people may think that setting goals is easy—that they simply need to state them. However, setting goals is hard work as well as one of the most important actions training managers can take to improve a training program's strategic focus. Setting a strategic goal should have the results of

- focusing the training manager, the training department's clients, and the training team on the target

- creating commitment and agreement about the training program's strategic goals.

In other words, strategic goal setting is a process of focusing the training department and WLP professionals on, as well as creating commitment and agreement about, the training function's direction. An effectively written strategic goal should have certain characteristics:

- *Specific:* The strategic goal should be so specific, well defined, and clear that anyone with basic knowledge of the training function can understand it and know what the training department is trying to accomplish.

- *Measurable:* To manage a training program to successful completion, training managers must be able to measure the goal. Every strategic goal can be measured; however, some goals can be measured more easily than others. In fact, developing clear, measurable standards for ambiguous and fuzzy goals is a good use of training managers' time. Without measurable goals, team members can't get a sense of direction. Some recommended standards for measuring any goal are quantity, quality, time, and cost. Each variable can be used in writing strategic goals that are measurable.

- *Agreed upon:* Agreement must exist on the program's strategic goals. Training managers' clients must agree that the end result should solve the problem or respond to the need that led to the initiative. The more people who agree and clearly understand the goal up front, the easier developing a plan of action for the training function's programs will be. This agreement also makes it easier to respond to changes that may require modifying the goal as the program unfolds.

- *Realistic:* Strategic goals must be realistic. All too often, WLP professionals set goals that are impossible to achieve, given the available resources and time. They set themselves and their programs up for frustration and failure. Making a goal realistic may mean adjusting the strategic goal, the deadline, or the resources.

- *Written:* All strategic goals should be written so that WLP professionals can better articulate desired outcomes for their program. Written goals improve commitment from training managers as well as their clients and help members of the training function stay focused during difficult economic times or stressful periods in the organization.

Objectives

WLP professionals use objectives to identify how to achieve their strategic goals. Objectives, the component parts of goals, break strategic goals down into sets of specific tasks. They indicate to each group or practitioner what to do, when to do it, and how to measure progress. In essence, objectives are subgoals of a strategic goal. Accomplishing all of the objectives leads to accomplishing the overall strategic goal.

Objectives focus on the details and tell training managers more about the specific tasks certain people need to accomplish. When creating objectives, a training manager can apply the same characteristics of strategic goals to each objective: specific, measurable, agreed upon, realistic, and written. If objectives don't meet these criteria, they can't guide WLP professionals' behavior effectively.

When training managers have written an objective, they need to identify key participants, resources, and inputs in achieving the objective. By identifying each objective with a specific group (or a specific person) and having a dialog about its formation, a WLP professional establishes ownership. Ownership leads people to take responsibility and feel committed to accomplishing the objective.

Clarifying strategic goals and objectives is essential for effective training programs and performance of professionals. Research on peak-performance people and groups suggests that they are always clear about their goals and objectives. They know where they are headed. This sense of direction substantially increases their chances of reaching their goals.

Action Plans

Creating an action plan is critical to the success of the strategic planning process. The actual steps in creating an action plan depend on the strategic goals and objectives that have been identified. Each action plan should, therefore, be tailored to those goals and objectives. For this reason, strategic goals and objectives must be written in such a way as to offer insight into the creation of an implementation plan.

An action plan should address two basic questions:

1. What are the possible problem areas in carrying out the strategic plan?

2. How will new strategies be developed if the main plan begins to go astray?

These are several important questions to answer while creating the action plan:

- How will the comprehensive strategic plan be implemented?

- Who will be in charge of implementing it?

- What is the basic timetable for implementation?

- How will the success of achieving the plan be measured?

- How will resources assigned to tasks work toward those objectives?

- What types of strategies can be used to motivate employees to achieve the objectives?

Phase 4. Evaluation

The last part of the strategic planning process is to evaluate or create a feedback system that provides information on the strategic plan's results. This step helps in learning how to design future strategic plans that are more focused and better targeted to accomplish a desired result. These are several important questions to ask when evaluating the plan or developing a feedback system:

- How will the WLP professional know when strategic goals and objectives have been accomplished?

- What type of early warning system can be created to flag impending problems?

- What alternative plans can training managers create if the initial plan fails?

- How can the WLP professional avoid punishing people if the plan fails?

- How will people be rewarded if they achieve goals and objectives successfully?

- How will the WLP professional monitor the progress of the strategic plan?

- Who will be in charge of checking on the strategic plan's implementation periodically?

- Is the feedback or evaluation system comprehensive enough to carry out future strategic plans successfully?

- Is the feedback or evaluation system designed in such a way that the WLP professional can use it in designing and developing future strategic plans?

At this point, WLP professionals need to review strategies, measure performance, and take corrective action when current strategies aren't leading to achieving established objectives.

The Role of the Training Manager

Depending on the type of organization, a training manager's role may vary quite a bit. A training manager acting as a one-person training department may be responsible for creating, delivering, sourcing and outsourcing, coordinating, funding, and evaluating the training the organization offers. At the other end of the spectrum, a training manager may have a large in-house staff and several vendor relationships to help meet all of the organization's needs. In this case, the training manager may spend time overseeing and focusing on future strategies that the training function needs to move toward and embrace.

All training managers, regardless of where they are on the spectrum, need to focus on

- creating value statements and defining their relationship to the corporate mission and vision

- determining how much (at least by percentage) of the organization's budget is spent on training

- communicating focus on individual needs rather than use of a blanket policy, such as stating that everyone must have 40 hours of training per year

- communicating value to the most senior levels of the training manager's organization and client organizations

- applying business acumen, including an understanding of the organization's current market share and profit-loss standing

- the organization's goals and progress toward those goals

- the processes and procedures for providing the organization's services or products

- external and internal forces that affect the company and the industry as a whole

- human motivation theories

- behavioral and industrial or organizational psychology
- technology
- accounting and financial concepts.

Accounting Terminology

To communicate the value of the training function credibly to senior management, the training manager must be able to use the language of senior management. The following list reviews some helpful accounting terminology:

- *Assets* refer to economic resources—in other words, what a company owns—that may be expressed in monetary terms.
- *Liabilities* are the debts or expenses a company owes.
- *Equity* is the value of the owners' or shareholders' portion of the business after all claims against it.
- *Balance sheet* is a statement of the firm's financial position, including assets, liabilities, and equity (liabilities + equity = assets).
- *Income statements* explain revenues, expenses, and profits over a specified period of time (revenues – expenses = net income).
- *Chart of accounts* is the listing of account lines maintained in the general ledger.
- *Cost-benefit analysis* is a comparison that weighs the costs of a training activity against the outcomes achieved and is carried out to determine the ROI.
- *Expenses* are the costs incurred in the process of earning revenues and conducting business.
- *Incurred expenses* are the expenses in which obligations have been fulfilled but not paid.
- *Operating expenses* are expenses that relate directly to business operations, not to providing products or services.
- *Revenue* is the money a company earns by providing goods or services to its customers.
- *Financial statements* are the four statements that show the end results of an organization's financial condition: balance sheet, income statement, statement of cash flows, and statement of owners' equity.

Budget Management

The budget process is especially critical to learning and performance functions. No matter where training is positioned in an organization, it serves as an organization-support function that gives the workforce the skills and knowledge it needs for business success. Because training is a support function rather than a revenue-producing function, training managers need to organize and run their departments like a business, demonstrating as much planning and fiscal responsibility as the parent organization. By running the training function like a viable business enterprise, a training manager gains credibility with business leaders and is able to command more responsibility in the organization.

Creating a good budget is more than an annual event designed to document spending; it's a working plan that guides fiscal decisions. A well-designed and -executed budget forms the foundation for developing next year's budget. Whether training is intended to correct past inadequacies or bring new expertise into the organization, understanding the value of the investment requires the financial data a budget supplies.

Although budgeting is often referred to as a process, in reality it's part of a larger accounting system. A typical accounting system includes three steps:

1. Budget design and development (forecasting)
2. Budget execution (expense tracking, monitoring, and management)
3. Reporting and reconciliation.

This process is circular. WLP professionals execute a budget within a specific window of time, normally a calendar year, and just before the yearly cycle closes, they begin again at step one, forecasting, designing, and developing a new budget for the next fiscal year.

In an optimal planning process, training managers design budgets based on the business plan, not on other factors, such as available revenue to fund the plan or previous spending levels. The assumption is that business goals justify the expenditures.

After a budget draft is completed, it typically goes through rounds of submissions and approvals, from the training manager's immediate supervisor up to various senior levels, depending on the organization's size. No matter how critical the funding need, unless the training manager presents the proposed budget in a logical, concise manner that documents how projects and programs link directly to the organization's success, it will be subject to revisions and budget cuts.

Preparing and managing budgets involves three major steps:

1. Prework research
2. Training plan processes
3. Budget management.

Step 1. Prework Research

Whether training managers are overseeing an existing training function or building the training function from scratch, spreadsheets with accounting codes can be daunting. Along with the training plan, these are other useful sources for gathering pertinent information:

- *Historical records:* Records of previous years' budgets help show trends. Some more stable accounts, such as audio and video or travel, may have a regular percentage increase every year. This information is a quick indication of how much to fund for those accounts.

- *Baseline funds:* Previous years' training activity records can give good information about funding amounts for baseline programs. If 12 "Introduction to Supervision" programs were offered each year for the past three years and the plan is to do the same next year, expenses for those programs are a matter of record and easy to pull together.

- *Budget accuracy:* WLP professionals can examine previous years' actual data to verify the accuracy of those budgets. If they budget $10,000 every year for travel yet never get approval to spend more than $5,000, the actual data provides a more accurate figure for next year's budget.

- *Benchmark data:* If the training department is new, the training manager may not have historical data, but external benchmark data can be used for funding information. ASTD has extensive benchmark data, cross-referenced by industry, size of organization, and other factors. Training managers can network with other training managers and use them as another source of information about program costs and expenses.

- *Postmortems:* Training managers conduct project postmortems to determine why projects succeeded or failed. Especially in program development projects, an inadequately funded development project may have lacked resources for proper instructional evaluation, adequate instructors, or other factors. This information aids in accurately budgeting for new development in the next year.

WLP professionals must remember that training never drives the budget process; finance does. Thoroughly researching successful budgets from outside the training function can be informative and helpful.

Step 2. Training Plan Processes

To develop a good, defensible budget, training managers often find it helpful to plan programs, projects, and events for the upcoming year. To do this, they need to create training plans. The annual training plan should include existing programs and services the learning function will continue to provide as well as propose new programs. Table 8-2 is a typical example of an annual training plan.

Starting the budget process with a clear training plan is a good idea and makes developing a budget fairly simple. Without a plan, this process may be reduced to guesswork on how to fund the various budget accounts. Without ties to the business, the amount of funds the training manager requests are subject to potential reduction and elimination. So what do training managers do to come up with a good plan? In most planning processes, they obtain information from two directions: from the top down and from the bottom up.

Table 8-2. Sample Training Plan

Program	Link to Business Plan	Length	Amount/ Frequency
HR policy overview	Supports organizational objective of reducing costs associated with employee turnover, lawsuits, and so forth	½ day	3 classes of 25, offered monthly
Performance management	Supports organizational objective of measuring and managing workflow, productivity, and business results	½ day	10 classes of 15, offered during the third quarter
Workplace harassment	Supports organizational value of fair and equitable treatment of all employees	2 hours	2 classes of 20, offered monthly

Gathering top-down information can sometimes be organizational detective work, depending on how much access the training manager has to high-level organizational data. Many organizations restrict the distribution of strategic plans or future forecasts for fear they'll end up in competitors' hands. As difficult as finding strategic information may be, however, it's critical for the future success of development efforts.

Bottom-up information is the needs assessment data and participant feedback gathered from clients. Because these requests often occur in reaction to current situations or crises, the training programs' focus in response to these needs tends to be more operational than strategic. Although bottom-up data is valuable, like top-down data, it should never be the sole source of information for a training plan. Not only does it tend to lack the long view, but it also frequently occurs in response to current crises.

Step 3. Budget Management

Training managers use charts, such as the one in table 8-3, as an easy way to track and manage budgets. The chart includes spaces for account codes and titles and makes it possible to track expenditures for each item.

Components of a Training Plan

Organizational elements: Training managers use these items representing the organizational strategic plan to show the link between the training plan and the organization's needs:

- organization's vision, mission, and value statements

- strategic goals

Table 8-3. Sample Chart of Accounts

Account Code	Description	Previous Year	Proposed	Variance Percentage	Variance Amount
1000	Salaries				
2000	Benefits				
3000	Professional services				
4000	Supplies				
5000	Transportation				
6000	Conferences and seminars				

- objectives

- organization's core competencies.

Training plan elements: To ensure that the learning function operates in a way that supports the business, training managers should link these items to organizational elements:

- training program titles

- **KSAs**

- program objectives

- competencies taught.

Training data needed for estimating program costs: Training managers should include the training data required to estimate program costs. These are examples of training data:

- duration (in days or hours)

- frequency (how many times taught per year)

- number of participants per class

- instructor costs

- travel expenses (for instructor and participants)

- facility costs (room rental, equipment rental)

- audiovisual costs (rental, purchase, maintenance)

- materials costs (workbooks, handouts)

- equipment costs (purchase or rental).

Budgets provide detail on accounts and amounts of forecasted expenses. Training managers might also need reams of backup documentation, but the actual budget is a simple total of line-item accounts and dollars. When the budget is approved, training managers need to track detailed information in expense logs, document details about deviations from the budget, and perform periodic budget reviews.

Budget Expenses

When developing a forecast and budget, training managers should consider training budget expenses, such as

- employee payments, including salaries, overtime pay, raises, and bonuses

- employee-related issues, such as costs for turnover, hiring and training new staff, and temporary employees to augment staff for special projects

- tools and equipment, including common items, such as lightbulbs, paper, binders, CDs, easel pad paper, markers, pens, and pencils

- new and replacement equipment, including any ongoing or annual maintenance renewals or service contracts

- training for trainers, including full-time new-hire staff and any vendor trainers (this expense should specify the number of train-the-trainer sessions expected and the number of different topics)

- travel, including travel for in-house staff and any vendor trainers

- facilities rental costs.

✓ Chapter 8 Knowledge Check

1. Which of the following is *not* one of the four phases of strategic plan development?

   __ **A.** Initiation

   __ **B.** Formulation

   __ **C.** Development

   __ **D.** Evaluation

2. In which phase of creating a strategic plan should a WLP professional conduct a SWOT analysis?

   __ **A.** Formulation

   __ **B.** Development

   __ **C.** Implementation

   __ **D.** Evaluation

3. How often should strategic planning occur?

   __ **A.** Once per year

   __ **B.** Once per quarter

   __ **C.** Monthly

   __ **D.** Continually and on an as-needed basis

4. Objectives are designed to help WLP professionals identify how to carry out which of the following?

   __ **A.** Mission

   __ **B.** Vision

   __ **C.** Strategic goals

   __ **D.** Action plans

5. During which of the following phases of strategic plan development does feedback and corrective action take place?

   __ **A.** Formulation

   __ **B.** Development

   __ **C.** Implementation

   __ **D.** Evaluation

6. **A training department with a large in-house staff and numerous vendor partners is in the process of developing a strategic plan. Given the size of the training department, what is the likely role of the training manager in the strategic planning process?**

___ **A.** Creating the training that supports the strategic plan

___ **B.** Delivering the training that supports the strategic plan

___ **C.** Evaluating the training that supports the strategic plan

___ **D.** Overseeing and focusing on future strategies for training

7. **Which of the following best describes a chart of accounts?**

___ **A.** A listing of account lines in the general ledger

___ **B.** An organization's economic resources expressed in monetary terms

___ **C.** An expense account that relates directly to business operations

___ **D.** One of the four primary financial statements filed annually by organizations

8. **Which of the following best describes an economic resource that may be expressed in monetary terms?**

___ **A.** Asset

___ **B.** Liability

___ **C.** Equity

___ **D.** Balance sheet

9. **Which of the following is *not* a source of prework research when forecasting a budget?**

___ **A.** Historical records

___ **B.** Participant demographics

___ **C.** Baseline funds

___ **D.** Benchmarking data

10. **Which of the following is a comparison that weighs the cost of a training activity against the outcomes achieved?**

___ **A.** Cost-benefit analysis

___ **B.** Chart of accounts

___ **C.** SWOT analysis

___ **D.** Income statement

11. An example of a budget expense includes all the following *except*

___ **A.** Salaries for full-time and temporary employees

___ **B.** Lightbulbs, flipcharts, tools, and equipment

___ **C.** Annual maintenance renewals or service contracts

___ **D.** Owner equity

References

Gilley, J.W. (1992). "Strategic Planning for Human Resource Development." *Infoline* No. 259206. (Out of print.)

Miner, N. (2001). "The One-Person Training Department." *Infoline* No. 250107. (Out of print.)

Oberstein, S., and J. Alleman. (2003). *Beyond Free Coffee and Donuts.* Alexandria, VA: ASTD Press.

Seagraves, T. (2004). *Quick! Show Me Your Value.* Alexandria, VA: ASTD Press.

Waagen, A.K. (2000). "How to Budget Training." *Infoline* No. 250007.

Younger, S.M. (1999). "How to Develop a Vision." *Infoline* No. 259107.

9
Principles of Management

An effective workplace learning and performance (WLP) professional must be both a dynamic leader who can inspire the team and an effective manager of the team and the team's resources. These professionals must possess or develop the ability to influence their employees, organizational leaders, and other employees. A training manager with exceptional leadership skills consistently demonstrates the leadership traits that the learning function teaches. The ability to influence others is essential to bring about the changes needed to keep the organization competitive and successful.

President Eisenhower used to demonstrate the art of leadership with a simple piece of string. Pull it, he'd say, and it'll follow you wherever you want; push it, and it will go nowhere. The same concept applies to leading people. Training managers don't automatically become leaders just because they have people working for them. If training managers have to force people to follow, they aren't leaders. Leadership is about getting people to follow someone's lead because they want to and often because they think it's their idea.

Successful leaders know that threats and reprimands don't work. Excellent leaders work to inspire people and make them want to cooperate. Managers who prod and goad rarely get the most out of people. Their employees do just enough to get by and keep the boss off their backs. The best leaders know that they get the most out of people by working with them, giving them the tools they need to do their jobs, and getting out of the way.

Most people want to do a good job and feel appreciated for it, but many managers are not good at showing appreciation. Although some people need to be pushed to do a good job, the need for excessive pushing indicates a lack of leadership. This chapter explores activities related to the training manager's role and key dimensions of management and leadership.

Learning Objectives:

☑ Discuss five activities the training manager is responsible for in ensuring that the training department helps the organization achieve its goals.

☑ Define the following functions of management and leadership: planning, organizing, coordinating, directing, controlling, and leading.

Training Manager Activities

In their role as managers, training managers are responsible for a number of activities, including

- providing vision, direction, values, and purpose to their employees
- motivating and inspiring people to work toward organizational goals
- planning and budgeting appropriately to reach organizational goals
- supervising the operations and staffing of the training department
- aligning people with departmental and business goals
- controlling issues and solving problems
- assessing training needs
- acting as an internal consultant.

Additionally, training managers must understand management and leadership principles.

Management and Leadership Functions

Training managers need to have some of the most important skills a leader can have: knowledge about finance, accounting, marketing, systems, procedures, structure, and supervision and control of employees. Leadership is more than management, however. It encompasses a set of 10 competencies organized into three categories:

Knowing themselves: Knowing their strengths and weaknesses includes qualities of

1. Self-awareness
2. Resiliency.

Working with others: This category includes many abilities identified as the biggest problems in organizations:

3. Interpersonal skills
4. Communication skills
5. Employee development
6. Vision creation and actualization.

Integrating self-knowledge with the ability to work with others: Integration, the most advanced form of leadership, is the ability to match the right person and skill set with the right job at the right time. This category includes

7. Customer orientation
8. Strategic business acumen
9. Project leadership
10. Change management.

The best leaders work to excel at these leadership functions encompassing a broad range of skills and competencies:

- *Planning:* Good leaders must be forecasters who can set goals and objectives; develop strategies; establish priorities; and be skilled at timing, sequencing, organizing, and budgeting. Planning involves establishing objectives and a course or direction for achieving them. Training managers also set product- or service-related goals, such as deciding to migrate three instructor-led courses to blended learning curriculums in the next year. Part of the planning process is breaking objectives down into subobjectives and action plans.

- *Organizing:* A good leader needs to design a structure to assist in goal accomplishment that relates human and nonhuman resources to the organization's tasks. Organizing involves dividing work into jobs, assigning those jobs to people, and delegating authority so that everyone can perform their jobs effectively. The key to effective organizing is teamwork and creating an environment of cooperation and understanding.

- *Coordinating:* Coordinating resources is a constant leadership task. It involves using all activities in the organization to give employees the resources and the means they need to accomplish goals.

- *Directing:* Leaders at all levels of the organization are responsible for making the right things happen. The purpose and the long-range goals help define what is right for a particular business. The most pertinent responsibility of a leader, at any level, is providing direction.

- *Controlling:* A leader must ensure that everything is performed and carried out according to plan, which involves evaluating or assessing situations. For example, training managers compare actual performance with ideal or expected outcomes and then try to resolve any meaningful differences to keep their operations aligned with the organization's plan. Some means of control that offer valuable feedback include the budget, quality control programs, and the training manager's own observations. Control information must be timely; if it's not received in time to take corrective action, the control system is inadequate.

- *Leading:* According to Kouzes and Posner (2003), leading requires the following traits: challenging the process, inspiring a shared vision, enabling others to act, modeling behavior, and encouraging organizational and individual outcomes.

✓　Chapter 9 Knowledge Check

1. **An organization recently went through a restructuring and several rounds of downsizing employees. Despite budget cuts, the training manager is still expected to deliver training to meet the current client base. Which of the following activities should take top priority in this situation?**

    __ **A.** Providing vision, direction, values, and purpose to employees

    __ **B.** Motivating, inspiring, and aligning people with departmental and business goals

    __ **C.** Supervising the operations and staffing of the training department

    __ **D.** Controlling issues and solving problems

2. **A training manager is upset with the performance review he just received from his director. The manager cannot understand what the problem is. He regularly works long hours six days a week doing everything from instructional design to setting up the training rooms. The director indicated the poor review was a result of numerous complaints from the manager's direct reports. Which of the following tasks is the manager likely not adequately focusing on?**

    __ **A.** Assessing training needs

    __ **B.** Budgeting and forecasting

    __ **C.** Providing vision, direction, values, and purpose to employees

    __ **D.** Delivering training

3. **To be a successful training manager, which of the following activities is most important?**

    __ **A.** Developing training programs

    __ **B.** Aligning people with departmental and business goals

    __ **C.** Double-checking to ensure everything is prepared for a training class

    __ **D.** Acting as the lead instructor for all mission-critical training programs

4. **Which leadership function is concerned with setting goals and objectives, developing strategies, and establishing priorities?**

    __ **A.** Organizing

    __ **B.** Planning

    __ **C.** Coordinating

    __ **D.** Directing

5. **Which leadership function is best described as ensuring that everything is performed and carried out according to plan?**

    __ **A.** Organizing

    __ **B.** Planning

    __ **C.** Coordinating

    __ **D.** Controlling

6. **A manager has received feedback that she needs to improve her planning skills. Which of the following activities should she focus on to better demonstrate her planning ability?**

    __ **A.** Dividing work into jobs and assigning those jobs to people

    __ **B.** Comparing actual performance with ideal or expected performance

    __ **C.** Enabling employees to do their jobs

    __ **D.** Establishing objectives and a direction to achieve them

References

Conover, D.K. (1996). "Leadership Development." *The ASTD Training and Development Handbook* (4th edition), R.L Craig, editor. New York: McGraw-Hill.

Kouzes, J.M., and Posner, B.Z. (2003). *The Leadership Challenge* (3rd edition). San Francisco: Josey-Bass.

Lyons, D.J., et al. (1985). "Business Basics." *Infoline* No. 258511. (Out of print.)

Patterson, J.G. (1994). "Fundamentals of Leadership." *Infoline* No. 259402. (Out of print.)

Russell, L. (2005). "Leadership Development." *Infoline* No. 250508.

10
Project-Planning Tools and Processes

Project-planning tools and processes are techniques that enable workplace learning and performance (WLP) professionals to serve on or lead the design team of a program development project. Project management principles provide the foundation for successfully completing a project through the processes of planning, organizing, and managing tasks, based on the elements of time, money, and available resources.

Project-planning tools, such as software, worksheets for planning and tracking, and project reports, support the processes of project management. During project planning, the project manager is solely responsible for gathering information needed to produce the **work breakdown structure (WBS)** and activity estimates and is also responsible for project staffing, resource leveling—addressing when too much work is assigned to one person by delaying or splitting up tasks—and the project schedule. During project execution, the project manager gathers status information from team members or team or project leaders and prepares project status reports.

People use the term *project management* frequently—and sometimes incorrectly. By definition, project management is planning, organizing, directing, and controlling resources for a finite period to complete specific goals and objectives. In the day-to-day work environment—where change is constant, competition between companies is lively, and new and better products are always needed—project management is one of the most efficient ways to deal with the ever-present challenges of increased costs and complexities, scarce resources, and constant improvements in technologies and methods.

Learning Objectives:

☑ Define the **project life cycle**, and discuss five phases within a life cycle.

☑ List four basic goals of project management.

☑ Describe each of the following roles within a project: sponsors, champions, managers, and team members.

☑ Describe the importance of time management in project planning.

☑ Explain the purpose of project planning worksheets.

☑ Define Gantt and **program evaluation review technique (PERT)** charts, and explain their use in project planning.

☑ Describe the purpose of project-planning software tools.

☑ List six project management issues.

Project Management

Whether developing new courses, adapting existing courses, finding the right self-paced solutions, rolling out training administration programs, or hiring the best external suppliers, training managers are constantly working on projects. Project management is critical, whether the training manager is working on a single project full time or working on multiple, complex projects, as is often the case.

What Is a Project?

The best place to start is to define the term *project*. A project has a distinct beginning and end. For example, developing a new course is a project. The WLP professional starts developing it on a particular day, and on another day, implements the course, enabling someone to learn from it. However, the WLP professional may also engage in an ongoing set of activities to maintain and enhance the course as it lives its useful life; those activities constitute a maintenance process, not a project. Ongoing activities without a specific endpoint are called processes. Table 10-1 shows the differences between projects and processes.

Processes can be redesigned and even removed; although they are important to a business, they don't really end. They are like clocks that keep running until their usefulness wears out. A project, in contrast, is the initial building block of that clock.

What Is Project Management?

Project management consists of planning, organizing, and controlling work. The goal of project management is to deliver a project that is on time, within budget, meets the required performance of specification level, and uses resources wisely. A project manager plans for a project's needs and then organizes and controls project resources as it progresses. This person has one foot in the future (creating a plan), one foot in the past (learning from mistakes), and the rest of the body in the present (reacting to surprises).

Project managers have a broad perspective; they watch the entire forest, not a specific tree. This is why being a project manager and a course developer at the same time is so difficult. A project manager keeps track of the gap between planned and actual time, cost, scope, and quality. A course developer, in contrast, focuses on creating the actual learning event. Each role has a distinct focus. The project manager and the course developer do *not* share priorities.

Table 10-1. Projects Versus Processes

Project	Process
Creating a one-day workshop	Mentoring an employee
Creating a web-based registration system	Administering training activities

Selecting a Project Manager

Does a training manager assign a project manager and then define the project, including goals and objectives, or does a training manager define the project first and then assign a project manager? No matter the order, both tasks need to happen. Ideally, the project manager comes on board before goals, objectives, and the plan are created because the project manager is ultimately responsible and accountable for project success.

Selecting the right person to be a project manager is important. Project managers must work constantly with change and deal with problems across functional areas. Their planning actions must be directed toward attaining the project's performance, cost, and schedule goals. A project manager's ability to get the job done through other people is another critical aspect of the job.

To choose a project manager, training managers normally scan an organization's employees to determine how successful each person has been with the performance of a particular functional group and who has had previous experience with similar projects. A training manager's responsibility, however, does not end with selecting and appointing a project manager. The training manager needs to provide the support and planning resources of the existing management structure, including a team of personnel from different functional areas, to accomplish the project objective.

Project Life Cycle

The project life cycle is everything that happens from the beginning to the end of the project. Organizations usually divide projects into several project phases to better manage and control project work. By managing projects in phases, project managers not only focus their time and energy on managing the current work but also look ahead to future phases. Together, the project phases are known as the project life cycle.

Each phase typically has one or more deliverables that must be completed to end one phase and move to the next. For example, when creating a new course, the design documentation should be completed and approved before beginning the development phase.

Depending on the industry and the type of work, the number and name of phases in the life cycle may vary. Table 10-2 shows an example of several phases and the types of activities a project manager may be responsible for in a project life cycle.

Defining the Project and Goals

Ideally, after the project manager is selected, the project team defines the project plan. The team may include members from functional areas. Team members provide a knowledge base for the project based on previous experience of similar projects, personnel resources, technology availability, or quality and control. These components help project managers define the proposed project.

Table 10-2. Sample Phases in a Project Life Cycle

Phase Name	Types of Activities
Conception	• Project idea is formulated. • Goals and objectives are defined and documented.
Selection	• Project manager is selected. • Project team members are assigned.
Planning	• Project manager and team develop the project plan. • Project manager plans the work and assigns resources to specific tasks. • Work is initiated.
Execution	• Project manager continues to plan the work for upcoming phases and works the plan for the current phase. • Project manager monitors the project schedule compared with the project plan and the baseline (what this person thought was going to happen and when, at the start of the project). • Project manager schedules resources and upcoming work. • Project manager authorizes the work and assigns resources to begin the work. • Project manager controls the scope, time, cost, and quality of project work.
Termination	• The project is formally closed out, including documenting best practices and lessons learned and filing all project information in a database or repository. • Project resources are released to functional departments or the next project team that needs to be staffed. • The work is transferred to ongoing operations or to whomever will maintain the project's end products.
Evaluation	• The organization conducts a formal review and evaluation of project goals and objectives and determines whether the project work and deliverables met the initial business need that gave rise to the project.

Regardless of the specific project goals and end deliverables, project managers are responsible for completing the project on time, within budget and scope, and to the quality specifications defined. These are their specific responsibilities:

- *Scope:* Ensuring that the project work, and only the approved project work, is completed. If any changes are requested or must occur, a formal scope change should be documented and approved by the appropriate project approver (for example, the sponsor).

- *Time:* Ensuring that the project schedule is planned, communicated, and monitored so that the work meets all milestones and deadlines.

- *Cost:* Tracking an initial project budget and expenses incurred as the project progresses to ensure that the project is delivered within budget.

- *Quality:* Measuring and monitoring that the project's product and deliverables meet the specified quality guidelines and standards.

- *Resource use:* Scheduling and managing the appropriate use of resources, including assigning the most qualified resources available to tasks and balancing the cost of resources assigned. (For example, contractors who have to work overtime may have much higher rates than internal employees.)

If a formal **project scope** change is approved, the project manager needs to adjust the project scope, time (project schedule), cost, quality, and resource use, as needed.

Project Planning

After the project team has discussed and agreed on a project's objectives, the project manager moves on to the next task: establishing a plan for how the project will be accomplished. These are the eight steps in this process:

1. Selecting a strategy for achieving the objective

2. Dividing the project's tasks into subtasks and units (WBS)

3. Determining the standards for measuring the accomplishment of each subtask (specifications)

4. Developing a time schedule and sequence for performing tasks and subtasks (**Gantt charts** and PERT charts—also known as the critical path method [CPM])

5. Estimating costs of each task and subtask and compiling the entire project's cost budget (if not determined)

6. Designing the staff organization needed to fulfill tasks and subtasks, including the number and kind of people required, their duties, and any necessary training

7. Developing policies and procedures that will be in effect during the project's life cycle

8. Acknowledging predetermined parameters imposed by the customer or organization, such as military standards or specifications.

The project manager then needs to carefully detail and document each element. Although there are many variations on the names of project life cycles, these models should generally align with the Project Management Institute (PMI) model (Duncan 1996).

A Project Management Glossary

These terms are common in the project management field:

Budget provides detail on financial or resource constraints under which a project operates. It should be divided to reflect major tasks to be performed, equipment or other material needs, and travel- or communications-related costs.

Critical paths identify the minimum time schedule for completing all of the tasks in a project with several tasks, some of them overlapping or depending on an earlier task.

Deliverables are the products to be delivered to the customer or client at the end of a project.

Gantt chart is a floating bar chart, or a series of lines, that represents the beginning and end dates for each task in a project, placed on some form of timeline.

Milestone is a key point (date) in a project when an event will occur.

PERT chart is a chart that illustrates the placement of cost-affecting elements and the interrelationship of activities and resources.

WBS shows a detailed subdivision of a project into tasks and subtasks to determine resources and schedules.

Source: Adapted from Conkright (1988).

Staffing a Project and Project Roles

During the planning process, a project manager compiles the tasks and subtasks that need to be performed. An important element of planning is finding and using the correct personnel to perform these tasks. Usually, in the interests of cost, time, and availability, a project manager can find the personnel for a project within the organization. However, project managers often have the option of hiring expertise from outside the organization; hiring a consultant, for example, may be the best way to obtain the required skills without hiring full-time employees.

When creating a project team, a project manager must consider many factors, including the current organizational structure, the commitment of management, the types of personnel needed, the number of hours needed to complete the project, other ongoing tasks for personnel, the cooperation of other line managers, and the informal lines of communication within the organization.

One method of developing a perfect team for a project is to compile a project summary sheet that describes the ideal qualifications for a specific task. With this summary sheet, a project manager can look at the available personnel in the functional organization and ascertain whether the people needed to do the job are current employees and whether they can be borrowed full time or part time for the duration of the project.

Many roles in an organization may influence a project—even though these roles may not be directly involved in carrying out the project's work. Project stakeholders include anyone with a vested interest in the project, which could include the public, company shareholders, and, of course, project team members. Stakeholders can make or break a project; they hold the keys to success. Because stakeholders are ultimately the judges of project's success, a project manager must constantly manage communications with them to make sure their expectations are appropriate. Table 10-3 outlines some stakeholder and project team roles.

Table 10-3. Stakeholder and Project Team Roles

Role	Description
Sponsor	The sponsor is often a member of senior management who supports the project's efforts to ensure success. The sponsor may report to other senior managers on the project's progress.
Champion	The champion communicates the project's benefits to the organization, helps remove barriers, and communicates the project's importance to stakeholders.
Budget client	This person controls the money. The budget client may or may not be the same person who requested the learning project but is the person who pays for it and the person whose signature is required for purchases. This person has the power to cancel the project at any time and is accountable for the project's cost and how it will provide a return to the business.
Business client	This person has requested the project or a subject matter expert (SME). For example, a manager having trouble with an employee might request the development of a one-day leadership workshop for that department. In many situations, business clients think they know what they want, but they may be unclear about what they need—or rather, what the business needs. Often, business clients have wrong or incomplete solutions, and the project manager and developers share responsibility for facilitating thoughts about the business problems and true needs.
Learners	Learners are people who have gaps in KSAs of which they may or may not be aware. Learners are the first people to evaluate the quality of the learning and provide feedback through words or behavior to business and budget clients. If the project manager and developer get input from learners throughout the development project, the results will be better aligned with the business need.

Table 10-3. Stakeholder and Project Team Roles, cont.

Role	Description
SMEs	SMEs fall into two general categories: Some have expertise in a specific skill, such as painting or electrical work, and are brought to a project to provide data for apprenticeship materials, procedural manuals, or another aspect of the project. Other SMEs have more conceptual or knowledge-based expertise, and the project is typically the result of research or experience gained in the field—or both. These SMEs are brought to a project to offer expertise in specialized areas.
Managerial roles	The project manager and other team leaders have to display various managerial roles on a project, including • interpersonal: builds team standards and fosters harmony • informational: gathers and disseminates information and helps team members communicate effectively • decisional: allocates resources, negotiates differences, and encourages project processes.
Team members	Team members are brought together for a specific project, usually based on knowledge or skills required for project success.

Time Management

Project time management includes the processes required to ensure timely completion of the project. According to the PMI (Duncan 1996), project time management includes these processes:

- *Activity definition* involves identifying the specific activities that must be performed to produce the project deliverables.

- *Activity sequencing* refers to identifying and documenting interactivity dependencies.

- *Activity duration estimating* involves estimating the number of work periods needed to complete each activity.

- *Schedule development* involves analyzing activity sequences, activity durations, and resource requirements to create the project schedule.

- *Schedule control* refers to controlling changes to the project schedule.

Although these processes are presented as discrete elements, they usually overlap and interact within project management. Several tools can be used to assist with project time management, including a WBS, a task list and Gantt chart, and network diagramming techniques, such as PERT and CPM.

Project Tools

A project manager uses several tools to help determine the tasks and amount of work, the timelines and key checkpoints, and the sequencing of tasks and duration. These tools include planning worksheets, WBS, Gantt charts, PERT charts, and software tools.

Planning Worksheets

A project manager is responsible for gathering background information about decisions that were made before gaining control of the project. Some resources to acquire this information include reviewing written documentation about the project, conducting interviews with people involved in the project, and conducting independent research that can supply useful background information.

After uncovering as much background information as possible, the project manager plans the project. Planning worksheets help develop a schedule, establish a budget, estimate costs, and draft a project charter or statement of work. A WBS, Gantt charts, and PERT charts are useful tools for identifying project tasks and subtasks, determining the duration of the work and schedules, and identifying required resources. With the assistance of the tools, project managers can use a variety of budget templates and estimation techniques to develop a project budget. A linear responsibility matrix, another spreadsheet-based tool, details team member assignments and roles—responsibility, accountability, participation, review—for each task.

Finally, project managers may use a project charter or statement of work to document understanding of the project and get approval to proceed. A typical project charter includes these sections: project purpose, deliverables, process and schedule, contact information, budget, assumptions, and approvals.

WBS

The primary tool to begin planning and documenting project deliverables is the WBS, which not only identifies tasks, subtasks, and units of work to be performed, but also assists in estimating and tracking costs of each of these elements.

A WBS represents a graphical hierarchy of the project, deliverables, tasks, and subtasks. As shown in figure 10-1, the top level of the WBS usually represents the project (for example, install air filter), the second level represents key deliverables (for example, build internal components, modify floor and roof, and inspect and test), and the subsequent levels show the tasks and subtasks required to complete the work.

Gantt Charts

A project's timeframe is derived from the plan and the WBS. The project manager lists the WBS components, arranges them in sequence, and determines how the elements mesh to form a milestone chart. Project managers should have some experience with

Figure 10-1. Sample WBS

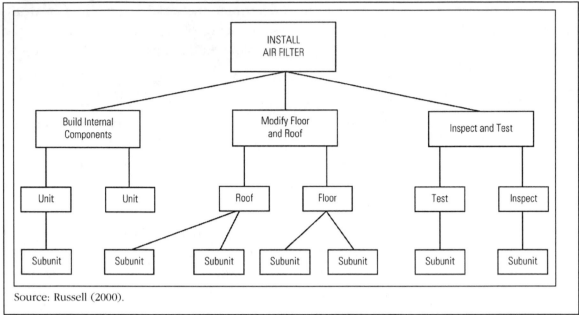

Source: Russell (2000).

similar activities to accurately estimate the time required to perform certain functions. Many project managers find it more realistic to plan time intervals as ranges rather than precise amounts of time.

Timeframe data is mapped into a chart called a Gantt chart (see figure 10-2), which graphically displays the time relationships of the project's steps and key checkpoints or deliverable dates, known as milestones. It's a valuable tool for project managers in planning, monitoring, and controlling projects.

Figure 10-2. Sample Gantt Chart

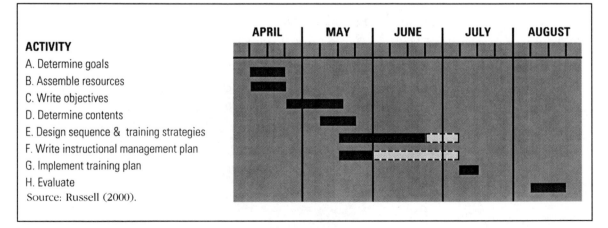

Source: Russell (2000).

PERT Charts

PERT and CPM charts are two widely used network-diagramming techniques. Network diagrams plot a sequence of activities (predecessor and successor tasks) to illustrate the interrelationships among activities and resources. PERT and CPM are also used to calculate the project duration. By completing this process, a project manager can determine the project's end date, total duration, and when the project must start to hit a certain deadline. These diagramming techniques also enable project managers to estimate a range of task durations by determining the optimistic, pessimistic, and most likely durations for each task. Figure 10-3 shows a sample PERT chart.

PERT charts display task, duration, and dependency information. Each PERT chart starts with an initiation node from which the first task originates. If multiple tasks begin at the same time, they all start from the node or branch or fork out from the starting point. Each task, represented by a line, shows the relationship among task dependencies (predecessor and successor tasks). Each task's duration is indicated on the diagram until all tasks are plotted through the end of the project (terminal node). This chart shows all tasks and indicates any slack time between the end of one task and the start of another. PERT charts may have multiple parallel or interconnecting networks of tasks.

CPM charts are similar to PERT charts and are sometimes known as PERT/CPM. A CPM chart indicates the critical path, which illustrates the path of tasks that together take the longest time to complete. Because tasks in the critical path take the most time, this path drives the project end date. Tasks on the critical path should receive special attention. For projects running behind schedule, project managers need to examine only critical path tasks to determine which tasks need more resources or to change sequencing to affect the project's end date.

Figure 10-3. Sample PERT Chart

ACTIVITY	DESCRIPTION	PREDECESSOR ACTIVITY	EXPECTED COMPLETION TIME (Weeks)
A	Determine goals	— —	2 (A)
B	Assemble resources	— —	2 (B)
C	Write objectives	A	3 (C)
D	Determine content	A, C	2 (D)
E	Design sequence & training strategies	A, C, D	5 (E)
F	Write instructional management plan	A, B, C, D, E	2 (F)
G	Implement program	A, B, C, D, E, F	1 (G)
H	Evaluate	A, B, C, D, E, F, G	2 (H)

Source: Russell (2000).

Software Tools

In today's automated environment, several software packages and computer systems make it possible for project managers to create automated Gantt charts, milestone charts, task lists, and resource assignments and to track project progress. These tools enable project managers to enter data for each element that can be tracked, make updates as schedules are adjusted, and add up costs and work-hour expenditures. Using a software package gives a project manager a source for actual versus projected charts for task performance and expenditures.

Project managers should investigate automated tools the company is using currently or packages they have experience with. Learning a new software management package in addition to trying to manage a project may be too much of an endeavor to handle at one time.

Although Gantt charts and milestone charts help planning by describing tasks and their associated timeframes, project managers may face some disadvantages if they rely solely on these tools to manage complex projects. For complex efforts, a project manager may also need computer-based network-analysis tools, such as PERT, CPM, and precedence diagramming method.

Network-based tools can be adapted to an organization's specific needs. Some of the most widely used applications

- communicate interdependencies and involvement of the project team
- estimate project length
- identify and resolve conflicts and bottlenecks
- simulate alternative plans of action
- accelerate project schedules
- determine optimum cost scheduling
- allocate resources
- manage cash flow.

A project manager should investigate currently available and known tools that will be the most helpful for completing the project. Gantt charts and network-based analysis methods are management tools; they are *not* substitutes for project management.

A major component of a project manager's job is planning and controlling costs. A project's success depends largely on correctly estimating the level of effort and expenditures required.

Project Management Considerations

A project manager should be aware of several elements on every project. Planning for these considerations proactively can mean the difference between success and failure on a project:

- **Scope creep:** The project scope is what will or won't be done on the project. Project scope management includes the processes needed to complete all required work (and only the required work) so that the project is completed successfully. Scope creep refers to the work or deliverables that are added to a project but were neither part of the project scope nor added through a formal scope change.

- *Timelines:* Timelines refer to the estimated duration of tasks and the project. By establishing project timelines early and communicating the work to be completed, a project manager proactively establishes the project schedule and measures and monitors the project plan for progress.

- *Milestones:* A milestone is a key point (date) in a project when an event will occur. By setting milestones, project managers can track when key events, such as deliverables or the end of phases, should occur. For example, training milestones might include completion and approval of the design plan, development of the instructor guide being 50 percent complete, pilot testing, or train-the-trainer sessions completed.

- *Project management software:* This class of computer applications is specifically designed to aid with planning and controlling project costs and schedules. Being a project manager doesn't mean sitting behind a computer and updating project management software. Most of a project manager's time should be spent communicating, planning, managing, and controlling the project and the schedule. Project management software assists with these activities; it doesn't replace them.

- *Resource identification:* Resource identification involves determining what resources (people, equipment, and materials) are needed, in what quantities, and when they are needed to perform project activities. A project manager may be responsible for creating a profile or job description to assist in identifying and staffing team members who have the required KSAs.

- *Resource management:* Project managers have many resources available to support a project, including people, equipment, and materials. If these resources are scheduled and used wisely, the project can run smoothly and cost effectively. If the project schedule is not optimized, some human resources, for example, may be overworked while others are underused.

- *Project status updates:* Project managers should spend approximately 80 to 90 percent of their time communicating. A project manager is the hub of coordination on a project. Project status updates with the client and the project team help keep the client's team and project team members informed.

- *Communication plan:* Communications planning involves determining the information and communication needs of project stakeholders. A project's success often depends as much on stakeholders and their perceptions as on the project manager and the work of team members. A stakeholder communication plan lays the groundwork for consensus and buy-in on an ongoing basis.

- *Training plan:* A project manager is responsible not only for staffing the project team, but also for developing individual and group skills to enhance project performance. A project team training plan should identify any KSA deficiencies and create a proactive plan to bridge the gaps through training.

- *Risk management:* Risk management is a subset of project management that includes the processes of identifying, analyzing, and responding to project risk. Risk management includes risk identification, risk quantification, risk response development, and risk response control.

- *Budget management:* Budget management includes the processes required to ensure that a project is completed within the approved budget, including resource planning, cost estimating, cost budgeting, and cost controlling. Project managers are responsible for identifying, monitoring, and controlling all project costs.

- *Key stakeholder management:* Managing stakeholder expectations may be difficult because stakeholders often have different objectives that may come into conflict. In general, differences among stakeholders should be resolved in favor of the customer or client. This doesn't mean disregarding the needs and expectations of other stakeholders; finding appropriate solutions to these differences can be one of the major challenges of project management.

- *Contingency or scenario planning:* When planning a project's scope, time, cost, quality, communication, and risk, the project manager should identify the most likely problems in each area and develop contingency plans. This what-if analysis helps project managers work through different scenarios to identify potential issues, adjust the project plan to mitigate the issues if possible, and have a plan in place if they do occur.

- *Barrier removal:* Because project managers are ultimately responsible and accountable for the project's success, they are also responsible for ensuring that the team has all resources needed to complete its tasks. When conflicts happen, resources aren't available, and so forth, it's the project manager's responsibility to solve the problems and remove the barriers so that the team can progress to accomplish project tasks within scope, on time, and within budget.

- *Celebration of successes:* Retaining project team members can be a key issue on long-term projects. Keeping employees motivated to continue to work through challenging projects with long hours is part of a project manager's job. At times, a project manager needs to lead communication on successes, such as meeting milestones, and celebrate those successes. In this way, a project leader shows team members that their efforts have made a difference and can keep them motivated to remain on the project and work through upcoming tasks and challenges.

✓ Chapter 10 Knowledge Check

1. **A fundamental technique of project management is planning projects in phases. All of the phases that represent the project from beginning to end are collectively called**

   __ **A.** Project scope

   __ **B.** Critical path

   __ **C.** Life cycle

   __ **D.** Conception

2. **Which of the following is *not* a standard phase name in the project life cycle?**

   __ **A.** Communicating

   __ **B.** Planning

   __ **C.** Execution

   __ **D.** Evaluation

3. **Which project phase is concerned with assigning resources to specific tasks and initiating the work?**

   __ **A.** Communicating

   __ **B.** Planning

   __ **C.** Executing

   __ **D.** Evaluating

4. **An example of a project management function is writing learning objectives.**

   __ **A.** True

   __ **B.** False

5. **Which of the following involves ensuring that all of the project work—and only the approved project work—is completed?**

   __ **A.** Scope

   __ **B.** Time

   __ **C.** Resource use

   __ **D.** Quality

6. Which of the following project team stakeholders and roles is defined as the person who controls the money and whose signature is needed to authorize purchases over a certain amount?

___ **A.** Sponsor

___ **B.** Champion

___ **C.** Budget client

___ **D.** Business client

---

7. Project time management includes processes required to ensure timely completion of the project. Which of the following is *not* a typical process used to support project time management?

___ **A.** Activity validation

___ **B.** Activity definition

___ **C.** Activity sequencing

___ **D.** Activity duration estimating

---

8. Which project management tool is used in planning and integrating the project and represents a graphical hierarchy of the project, deliverables, tasks, and subtasks?

___ **A.** WBS

___ **B.** Gantt chart

___ **C.** PERT chart

___ **D.** Milestone chart

---

9. A project manager has been assigned to a new project and has finished collecting information. She is now developing several planning worksheets. Which of the following is she most likely creating?

___ **A.** Process map

___ **B.** SWOT analysis

___ **C.** Strategic plan

___ **D.** Gantt chart

---

10. Which of the following represents the minimum time schedule for completing all tasks in a project and drives the project's end date?

___ **A.** Deliverables

___ **B.** Milestone

___ **C.** Critical path

___ **D.** Gantt chart

11. A project manager is in the process of mapping the timeframe data for the project within a chart, which graphically displays the time relationships of the project's steps and deliverable dates. Which of the following is the project manager developing?

___ **A.** WBS

___ **B.** PERT chart

➘ **C.** Gantt chart

___ **D.** CPM chart

---

12. With the arrival of software tools such as automated Gantt charts and network-based analysis methods, the position of project manager is no longer necessary.

___ **A.** True

➘ **B.** False

---

13. Which of the following is best defined as work or deliverables that are added to a project but were not part of the initial approved plan nor added through a formal change?

___ **A.** Scope

___ **B.** Milestones

___ **C.** Deliverables

➘ **D.** Scope creep

References

Conkright, T.D. (January 1988). "So You're Going to Manage a Project. . . ." *Training*, pp. 62–67.

Duncan, W.R. (1996). *A Guide to the Project Management Body of Knowledge.* Newton Square, PA: Project Management Institute.

Modell, M.E. (1996). *A Professional's Guide to Systems Analysis.* New York: McGraw-Hill.

Russell, L. (2000). *Project Management for Trainers.* Alexandria, VA: ASTD Press.

Thompson, C. (1990). "Project Management: A Guide." *Infoline* No. 259004.

Toenniges, L., and K. Patterson. (2005). "Managing Training Projects." *Infoline* No. 250512.

11
Communication and Influence

 Training managers are under increasing pressure to deliver solutions better, faster, and cheaper but with the same successes that other more well-funded programs previously implemented. Training managers are expected to interface with executives and clearly articulate how the learning function can help the organization to accomplish the stated business goals and objectives. They are also expected to direct and monitor the work performed by staff members, manage projects and budgets, implement new systems, and show the strategic value that the learning function provides.

All training manager roles require a mastery of an array of management skills, from communicating (written and verbal) and coaching to public speaking and managing people. Producing effective written communications—proposals, executive summaries, important emails—is more crucial than ever. For training managers to influence the organization with regard to vision and initiatives, they must be able to customize a message, read and react to an audience's body language, facilitate question-and-answer sessions, skillfully handle tough questions, and deliver memorable messages that audiences will act on.

How do training managers do all of this? When training managers understand what another person is saying, they can use verbal communication skills to determine the best course of action. By asking open-ended questions, the training manager can shape the course of the conversation, get an understanding of the larger needs, and help other people understand their own positions. Using closed-ended questions allows training managers to get to the core elements of the other person's viewpoint.

Another vital aspect of training managers' communication skills is the ability to speak before large and small groups. Workplace learning and performance (WLP) professionals must always be prepared before making any presentation, anticipate questions that will be asked, and think of ways to enhance the presentation through visual aids. Those skills help WLP professionals regardless of the situation, whether they are conducting an employee's performance appraisal or asking executive staff to increase the learning function's budget by 15 percent.

The rate at which a typical speaker talks (about 140 words per minute) and the rate at which a listener can understand (from about 280 to 560 words per minute) are exploited by TV and radio commercials, which use electronically altered speech to tell and sell listeners more. Some speakers, such as auctioneers, talk at a rate of speed much faster than the average listener can comprehend. With practice, even this fast-talking style can be understood, however. Most people can think three times faster than the person sending the message.

Learning Objective:

☑ Explain why communication and influencing are critical skills for a training manager.

Key Knowledge: Communicating Strategies

The first step in effective communication is deciding what to communicate to someone. A WLP professional can begin by making a list of items to be addressed and then formulate fuller ideas based on those items. Making sure there are logical segues between conversation points helps communication flow in a more orderly way. If information about a change is communicated in an unmanaged fashion, it becomes diffused, less specific, and interpreted in arbitrary ways. Problems occur when people say one thing, but their behavior or actions suggest the opposite. Professionals must be true to their word when communicating—that's the most important aspect of communicating effectively.

When communicating change initiatives to others, three points help ensure that all involved understand:

1. *Telling them in advance:* People don't like surprises, so springing an unexpected change on employees can create a sense of panic. People need to know in advance that a change is coming so that they have time to prepare.

2. *Giving enough information:* Vague language should be avoided in communication. If training managers are unclear, they should wait until all points are clear before communicating them to someone else.

3. *Ensuring that messages correspond with actions:* Also called "walking the talk," making sure verbal or written communiqués are reflected in subsequent actions is imperative in business communications.

For more information, see Module 5, *Facilitating Organizational Change,* chapter 9, "Communication Theory."

12
Human Resources Systems

Regardless of where in the organizational chart the training function resides, workplace learning and performance (WLP) professionals should be aware of how human resources (HR) systems integrate with their success, and vice versa. One area in which WLP professionals may have a role is recruitment. A successful employee–employer relationship begins with hiring the right person. To achieve that aim, a WLP professional may need to give hiring managers training on interviewing candidates. In this role, a WLP professional needs to be aware of laws and legal decisions that can affect hiring procedures (more details on legal issues are covered in chapter 15).

A WLP professional should also be aware of how the training function relates to HR development. Facets of this development may include on-the-job training, performance objectives and appraisal, and links to organizational goals.

Learning Objectives:

- ☑ List six components of a HR system and what each does.

- ☑ Discuss how the training function interfaces with an organization's HR system.

- ☑ Explain how employee-related activities, including developmental planning, management by objective, job responsibilities, and compensation systems, are used to link individual goals with organizational goals.

HR Systems

Planning for the learning function in an organization doesn't happen in a vacuum. Training is a core component of ***human resource development (HRD)*** that integrates with several other HR functions, including recruitment and selection, compensation, performance management, reward management, and job design.

Recruitment and Selection

In the training industry, when WLP professionals talk about building organizational capacity, they mean developing a talented workforce to meet business and customer needs. For many organizations, attracting and retaining the right talent is their primary business need. To attract prospective employees, businesses have begun offering many perks, such as stock options, flexible working hours, on-site child care, and fitness centers. Organizations realize that employees leaving the organization can cause an intellectual drain, and losing talented people has serious implications. Some calculations indicate that the cost of losing one employee is approximately one and one half times that person's annual salary.

So how can training help with recruitment and selection? According to Wagner (2000), studies have shown that American workers who receive employer-sponsored training are more satisfied with their jobs and more likely to stay with their employer than those who don't. A 1999 Kepner-Tregoe report found that the top three reasons employees left their organizations were perceived lacks of financial rewards, recognition, and career development. The bottom line: If employees don't receive training at their current workplaces, they will go elsewhere.

Compensation

In *Keeping the People Who Keep You in Business,* Leigh Branham (2001) reviews the role money plays in retaining the right people. He explains that although surveys rank pay behind factors such as meaningful work, meeting challenges, and opportunity for advancement, compensation places people in a socioeconomic niche. It determines what they can and can't buy, which makes compensation an emotional and important issue.

Training managers should look at compensation not as a way to drive performance, but as a message to employees about what results they value. Branham (2001) notes that in 2000, about two-thirds of small and medium companies offered some kind of variable pay, such as profit sharing or bonus awards, to their employees, compared with less than 50 percent in 1990.

Four links need to connect performance and rewards: measurement of valuable results, accomplishment of results, accomplished results being rewarded, and rewarded results being valued. Many organizations switch to variable pay options, such as the following examples, as a way of updating compensation practices:

- *Special recognition monetary awards* provide cash payouts to recognize unplanned, significant individual or group contributions that far exceed expectations.

- *Individual and group variable pay* is designed primarily for employees or teams who don't normally participate in incentive compensation programs, such as technical support, or for positions that have little or no interaction with others.

- *Lump sum awards* are used to reward individual employee performance when base pay is already above the competitive market rate for the job. This option allows organizations to reduce annual payroll yet still reward top performers.

- *Stock options* offer employees the opportunity to purchase for-profit common stock at some time in the future at a specific price. Stock options serve to tie employees to the organization because ownership tends to cause employees to be more aware of how their organization is performing.

Performance Management

Employees want to be recognized for the jobs they were hired to do. Achieving business goals is a critical success factor for any organization, and organizations realize that the means to this end rests with performance of the workforce.

Performance management has often been described as the process of developing, motivating, deploying, and aligning people to increase business performance. To aid in this process, performance management systems are computer-based systems that HR uses to understand which employees need to develop required skills and expertise.

One of the biggest obstacles that hinders performance management is a lack of process and systems integration—leaving HR unable to link data or provide executive access to key information. For the HR department to truly add value to the organization, HR initiatives must be tied to business results and support the achievement of outcomes and metrics.

Reward Management

Cash bonuses are appreciated, but they certainly aren't the only way to reward employees. Other methods can be equally as effective. There are two keys to rewarding employees. First, WLP professionals must understand the basic needs that motivate employees. Second, they must monitor employees continually to determine whether their needs are being met.

In the *Manager's Desk Reference,* Cynthia Berryman-Find and Charles B. Fink (1996) state that 99 percent of employees are motivated by one of these seven needs: achievement, power, affiliation, autonomy, esteem, safety and security, and equity (being treated fairly). Some ways to recognize which need is the primary motivator for employees include considering their personality type based on personality inventories, listening empathetically, or simply asking questions about job satisfiers.

Job Design

J.R. Hackman and G.R. Oldham's (1975) job characteristics model explains in detail how to make jobs more interesting and motivating for employees. In this model, every job has five characteristics that determine how motivating workers will find it. These characteristics determine how employees react to their jobs and lead to outcomes such as high performance and satisfaction and low absenteeism and turnover:

1. *Skill variety* is the extent to which a job requires an employee to use a wide range of skills, abilities, or knowledge. For example, the skill variety for a research scientist is higher than what's required of a food server.

2. *Task identity* is the extent to which a job requires a worker to perform all of the tasks necessary to complete that job from the beginning to the end of the production process. For example, a crafts worker who transforms a piece of wood into a custom-made piece of furniture has higher task identity than a worker who performs only one of the numerous operations required to assemble a television.

3. *Task significance* is the degree to which a worker believes the job is meaningful because of its effects on people inside the organization (such as co-workers) or outside the organization (such as customers). For example, teachers who see the effect of their efforts in well-educated and well-adjusted students enjoy high task significance compared with a dishwasher who monotonously washes dishes as they come into the kitchen.

4. *Autonomy* is the degree to which a job gives an employee the freedom and discretion to schedule different tasks and decide how to carry out those tasks.

5. *Feedback* is the extent to which performing a job gives workers clear and direct information about how well they completed the job.

Hackman and Oldham (1975) argue that these five characteristics influence an employee's motivation because they affect three critical psychological states. If employees believe their work is meaningful and that they are responsible for outcomes and for knowing how those outcomes affect others, they will find the work more motivating; be more satisfied; and, therefore, perform at a high level.

Training and Development

In the 21st century, few doubt the wisdom of the observation that the only constant is change. Changing economies, changing geographical realities, and changing technologies are a triple threat to everyone's adaptability. That threat exists on every level: personal, professional, and corporate.

Only by responding to current challenges and preparing for the future can an organization and the learning function be increasingly valued players. To support organizations' long- and short-term business goals, training managers should learn the overriding philosophy of the business and review the current scope of training operations. Training managers also need to look long and hard at programs and policies that are needed for the HR department to be responsive to changes occurring inside and outside the organization.

As the changing business world requires increasingly complex job skills and demands adaptability to new job functions and technology, the challenge of recruiting and retaining skilled workers also increases. The advantages of forecasting five to 10 years ahead require ongoing examination of a corporate strategy roadmap and marshaling skills and resources that the HR department needs to deliver skill sets training. Training managers should try to look down the road to make decisions within two years about developing the training programs that will be needed in five to 10 years. Simultaneously, they need to provide employees with the tools and training that fit the situation and the organization they will deal with in the near future.

In an ever-changing environment, one competitive advantage is knowledge. When markets shift, technologies proliferate, competitors multiply, and products become obsolete almost overnight, successful companies are those that consistently create knowledge, disseminate it throughout the organization, and quickly embody it in new technologies and products. The training department and HR organization need to find ways to track and account for knowledge as an asset because it's an essential ingredient for rapidly changing times and innovation. The workforce produces intellectual capital when the application of ideas or skills produces higher-value assets—often new assets and opportunities of enormous value.

Because the primary process of HR development is locating and preparing the appropriate knowledge and skill sets, the primary outcome that HR and the organization want is efficient, useful application of that knowledge. The business of helping people use their brains better is the business and capital of training and development.

Employee-Related Activities

Within the organization, training departments and HR can use several strategies and tools to help motivate employees and drive desired behaviors, including

- performance-based budgets linked to individual outcomes
- behavior and competency assessments
- development planning in the form of training plans
- management by objective
- job responsibility and KSA evaluation
- components of the performance improvement process, including individual feedback
- links to the compensation system to ensure that the organization is motivating desired behaviors
- balance with meeting organizational goals and objectives.

✓ Chapter 12 Knowledge Check

1. **Reward management is primarily concerned with strategies using monetary compensation to drive employee performance.**

   ___ **A.** True

   ___ **B.** False

2. **Performance management is primarily concerned with which of the following processes?**

   ___ **A.** Developing, motivating, deploying, and aligning people to increase business performance

   ___ **B.** Continually monitoring employees and providing feedback to increase their performance

   ___ **C.** Attracting and retaining the right talent to increase business performance

   ___ **D.** Retaining the right people through pay grades and compensation systems to increase performance

3. **Which of the following is a computer-based system that HR professionals use to understand which employees need to develop required skills and experience?**

   ___ **A.** Performance management

   ___ **B.** Reward management

   ___ **C.** Succession management

   ___ **D.** Job management

4. **The HR department of an organization is designing several new jobs. One of the goals of the design team is to develop jobs that employees will find interesting and motivating. Altering which of the following job factors is *least* likely to affect employee motivation?**

   ___ **A.** Skill variety

   ___ **B.** Compensation

   ___ **C.** Task identity

   ___ **D.** Autonomy

5. **Training managers are responsible for helping the HR department plan short- and long-term goals based on changes occurring inside and outside the organization.**

   ___ **A.** True

   ___ **B.** False

6. **Within the organization, training managers can use several strategies and tools to help motivate employees and drive desired behaviors. Which of the following is *not* one of those strategies or tools?**

__ **A.** Performance-based budgets linked to individual outcomes

__ **B.** Realigning the organization, departments, and job roles frequently

__ **C.** Management by objective

__ **D.** Development planning in the form of training plans

7. **It is the responsibility of the training function, not necessarily the HR department, to forecast future training needs.**

__ **A.** True

__ **B.** False

8. **Compensation and reward systems are the best way to retain the best employees.**

__ **A.** True

__ **B.** False

9. **Conducting periodic job responsibility and KSA evaluations helps to accomplish which of the following objectives?**

__ **A.** Motivate employees

__ **B.** Drive desired behaviors

__ **C.** Link individual goals with organizational goals

__ **D.** All of the above

References

Berryman-Find, C., and C.B. Fink. (1996). *The Manager's Desk Reference* (2nd edition). New York: AMACOM.

Branham, L. (2001). *Keeping the People Who Keep You in Business*. New York: AMACOM.

Hackman, J.R., and G.R. Oldham. (1975). "Development of the Job Diagnostic Survey." *Journal of Applied Psychology*, volume 60, pp. 159–170.

Lauby, S. (2005). "Motivating Employees." *Infoline* No. 250510.

Sandler, S.F., editor. (July 2005). "The Latest Business Focus for HR: Workforce Performance Management." *HRFocus* 28, pp. 3–4.

Stolovitch, H.D., and E.J. Keeps. (2002). *Telling Ain't Training*. Alexandria, VA: ASTD Press.

Wagner, S. (August 2000). "Retention: Finders Keepers." *T&D*, p. 64.

Wiggenhorn, W.A. (1996). "Organization and Management of Training." *The ASTD Training and Development Handbook* (4th edition), R.L. Craig, editor. New York: McGraw-Hill.

13
Business Model, Drivers, and Competitive Position

Workplace learning and performance (WLP) professionals need a basic understanding of the way businesses function in their organization's community and industry, the way funding and revenues are determined, and the strategic strengths and weaknesses of the business. In addition, they need to be able to convey learning initiatives and solutions in the terminology of their organizations to give the learning function credibility as a strategic business partner.

Developing and managing a strategic learning process is nearly impossible without first becoming a strategic partner in the organization. To become a strategic partner, training managers should focus on

- providing services that support the organization's business strategy

- improving the visibility of the learning function's activities and accomplishments

- measuring results or at least tying results to other internal measures

- becoming educated in strategic planning

- educating others in the strategic planning process.

Learning Objectives:

☑ Discuss how understanding the state of the business is imperative for a WLP professional to help the organization achieve its goals.

☑ Define what is meant by the culture or value system in an organization.

☑ List four environmental factors that affect an organization.

State of the Business

As defined by Wikipedia, "a business model, also called a business design, is the mechanism by which a business intends to generate revenue and profits. It is a summary of how a company plans to serve its customers. It involves both strategy and implementation and involves the totality of how a business

- selects its customers
- defines and differentiates its product offerings
- creates utility for its customers
- acquires and keeps customers
- goes to the market (promotion strategy and distribution strategy)
- defines the tasks to be performed
- configures its resources
- and captures profit."

Business models vary by industry and in complexity and describe how an organization functions. Defining the type and state of the business helps determine whether it will be successful. In a now classic example, railroad companies defined themselves as being in the railroad business rather than the transportation business. Had they answered the question "What is your business?" differently, they might have emerged as an exploding growth industry instead of a declining, or, at best static, part of the transportation industry. The same is true when WLP professionals define the business and the state of the business in relation to its competition.

The learning function will have trouble becoming a valued business partner if the training manager doesn't understand the

- business model
- business objectives
- factors that affect growth
- strategic business drivers for the organization and the industry
- corporate success measures.

An organization's business objectives state what the organization wants to accomplish. For example, a business objective might be to increase the profitability by 5 percent in the next year with the launch of a new product.

Several factors may also affect organizational growth including the competitive environment and the industry as well as the current culture and values of an organization.

Business drivers are the internal and external forces that direct an organization's strategy, goals, business needs, and performance needs. An example of an external business driver is government; regulation or deregulation forces changes in competition or the overall business environment. An example of an internal business driver is technology;

new innovations in technology create opportunities or needs for changes in information storage and processing.

To complete the picture of the state of the business, WLP professionals also need to understand corporate success measures and how the organization defines and measures success. All of these factors drive how the learning function creates and links training programs to business goals and objectives.

For more information, see Module 3, *Improving Human Performance,* chapter 2, "Business, Performance, and Gap Analysis," and Module 4, *Measuring and Evaluating,* chapter 1, "Theories and Types of Evaluation."

Culture or Value Systems

After WLP professionals have defined the big-picture perspective on the state of the business, goals, and objectives and how success is measured in the organization, they should examine the organization's culture and value systems. An organization's culture—the assumptions employees share about their work and their feelings toward the organization—can't be ignored. Assessing the culture and the degree to which it helps or hinders deployment of a strategic plan is critical to the plan's success.

Conducting an environmental scan to proactively assess the effect of change on the organization highlights environmental trends and forces—both current and future—leading to shifts in strengths and weaknesses and new opportunities or threats. To understand culture and value systems in the organization, training managers should consider

- company history

- mission and goals

- strategy, tactics, vision, and plans.

For additional information about business objectives, see Module 5, *Facilitating Organizational Change,* chapter 5, "Systems, Culture, and Leadership in an Organizational System."

Environmental Factors

To become a strategic partner and valued member of the organization, training managers must understand environmental factors and the influence they have on an organization:

- *Internal factors* include technology; new products; shareholder or financial influence; and changes in systems, processes, or policies. Examples include changes in systems, processes, or policies may require changes in employee skills or behavior.

- *External factors* include economic changes, human resource and skill shortages, governmental decisions, public perception, and market or customer requirements. Examples include upturns or downturns in the economy, embargoes or trade restrictions, and other economically driven situations.

- *Employee factors* include shortages in the number of employees or in the number of employees with a certain skill set, union demands, and employee needs to balance family and work relationships.

- *Contractual factors* include contracts for full- or part-time employees and vendor agreements for services and raw materials.

Organizational Structure

Organizational structures help define department functions; roles and responsibilities; relationships among departments; reporting structures; the organizational layout, flow, and exchange of information, documents, and other resources; and the workflow network, the formal organizational structure supporting the workflow for business processes and delineating how each process works.

To help facilitate the flow of information in knowledge in an organization, **knowledge exchanges**, also known as knowledge exchange networks, enable different groups in an organization to share documents and information on products to create lists of links in simple web pages and discuss issues of mutual interest. Knowledge exchanges are restricted to members within an organization or to designated community members, such as external project team members or vendors.

Knowledge exchanges try to leverage the fact that much of the knowledge in an organization lies in the heads of its staff rather than in databases. These knowledge exchanges and communities are, therefore, a natural place to seek out and access specialized knowledge.

For more information, see Module 8, *Managing Organizational Knowledge,* chapter 5, "Business Process Analysis," and chapter 7, "Information Architecture."

✓ **Chapter 13 Knowledge Check**

1. **Organizational structures help to define department functions, roles and responsibilities, relationships among departments, reporting structures, and the flow of information.**

   __ **A.** True

   __ **B.** False

2. **A business model is defined as a mechanism by which a business intends to generate revenue and profits and involves both the strategy and the implementation for defining product offerings, acquiring and keeping customers, the marketing strategy, and how it configures revenue and generates profit.**

   __ **A.** True

   __ **B.** False

3. **Strategic business drivers are defined as**

   __ **A.** Internal and external forces that affect the organization's culture and values and the need to facilitate change within an organization

   __ **B.** Internal and external forces that affect the knowledge, skills, and information in the organization and determine learning needs of individuals

   __ **C.** Internal and external forces that affect an organization's revenue, expenses, and expected profitability

   __ **D.** Internal and external forces that affect an organization's strategy, goals, business needs, and performance needs

4. **An organization's culture is defined as the assumptions employees share about their work and feelings toward the organization.**

   __ **A.** True

   __ **B.** False

5. **A training director new to the company spends much of his first few weeks learning about the company's history, mission, goals, strategy, tactics, vision, and plans. This information will help the new director understand which of the following?**

   __ **A.** Company's culture

   __ **B.** Department's budget

   __ **C.** Training group's strengths

   __ **D.** Training group's weaknesses

6. **Assessing an organization's culture is *not* required for successfully implementing most small initiatives.**

    __ **A.** True

    __ **B.** False

7. **Which of the following environmental factors includes technology, new products, and changes in systems processes or policies?**

    __ **A.** Contractual

    __ **B.** External

    __ **C.** Employees

    __ **D.** Internal

8. **Which of the following environmental factors includes economic changes, HR, and skill shortages?**

    __ **A.** Contractual

    __ **B.** External

    __ **C.** Employees

    __ **D.** Internal

9. **A director of a training department is criticized by company leadership for "signing off" on poor training vendor agreements. Which of the following environmental factors is this director not adequately managing?**

    __ **A.** Contractual

    __ **B.** External

    __ **C.** Employees

    __ **D.** Internal

10. **A small consulting firm has more work than it can deliver. Although the firm has tried to hire additional consultants, no qualified candidates can be located. Which of the following environmental factors is negatively affecting this company?**

    __ **A.** Contractual

    __ **B.** External

    __ **C.** Employees

    __ **D.** Internal

References

Barksdale, S., and T. Lund. (2001). *Rapid Needs Analysis.* Alexandria, VA: ASTD Press.

Larsen, N.G. (2002). "Implementing Strategic Learning." *Infoline* No. 250210.

Lyons, D.J., et al. (1985). "Business Basics." *Infoline* No. 258511. (Out of print.)

Verardo, D. (1997). "Managing the Strategic Planning Process." *Infoline* No. 259710.

Wiggenhorn, W.A. (1996). "Organization and Management of Training." *The ASTD Training and Development Handbook* (4th edition), R.L. Craig, editor. New York: McGraw-Hill.

Wikipedia contributors. (2006). "Business Model." http://en.wikipedia.com/wiki/business_model.

14
External Systems

External systems are just one factor that influences the culture of an organization and affects its business trends. The influences of external systems emerge on two levels: external environmental factors and external relationships. Understanding these factors and their influence in an organization is beneficial to workplace learning and performance (WLP) professionals because it provides insight for developing and delivering training. Some factors may be more influential than others, but having an awareness and understanding of them allows WLP professionals to identify trends affecting the organization's needs and learners.

Different external environmental factors can affect an organization at different times and to different degrees, depending on the type of business. Some factors have more of an effect at a higher level in the organization, including political factors, economic factors, sociological or cultural trends, and global issues. Other external environmental factors, such as technology changes and employment trends, have an effect on both the organization and employees.

External relationships influence an organization on a smaller scale, relating to its customers, vendors, competitors, community, charities, and employees. Those same factors affect employees more directly through their interactions on both business and personal levels.

Being aware of the factors affecting an organization is critical in understanding the needs of a business and its sources. Understanding the sources of organizational needs and their influence on training trends leads WLP professionals to identify next steps in developing appropriate programs.

Learning Objectives:

☑ List and define six environmental factors that affect an organization.

☑ List six external relationships that affect an organization, and describe how they affect the learning needs of employees either positively or negatively.

External Environmental Factors

To become a strategic partner and valued member in the organization, training managers must understand external factors that affect the organization, including politics, the economy, society, culture, global factors, technology, and employment. Conducting an environmental scan and a strengths, weaknesses, opportunities, and threats analysis helps WLP professionals understand the current environment and gain more insight into the corporate strategic plan, which defines where the organization aims to be in the future.

An environmental scan is an inventory of the political, economic, sociological, cultural, global, technological, and employment forces that influence the way an organization functions. These factors relate to both internal and external influences, such as employees and contractual issues. The scan involves analyzing the current environment and the trends that may affect it and assessing customer needs and stakeholder expectations. There's no magic formula for conducting environmental scans, but WLP professionals should strive to get as much information as possible on these factors that could influence the direction of an organization:

- *Economic factors* include effects of employment rate and interest rates on the gross domestic product, consumer price index, disposable income, and inflation.

- *Political influences* include level of privatization in governmental services, political trends affecting suppliers and customers, and level of partisanship in governmental bodies.

- *Sociological factors* include worker skills, corporate responsibilities and ethics, population shifts, immigration, migration, age, gender, generational differences, minority groups, and nontraditional labor.

- *Cultural influences* include effects of national and local cultures on employees and organizations as well as corporate cultures on departmental, regional, and organization-wide levels.

- *Global influences* include effects of multinational organizations (such as the European Union), wage comparisons, trade agreements, and globalization.

- *Technological factors* include effects of advances in technology on skills and process changes.

- *Employment factors* include effects of recruitment and unions on unemployment, turnover, and relocation.

External Relationships

Partnerships, which represent one type of external relationship that can have an enormous effect on organizations, range from formal customer–client agreements to informal networks and take many forms. Training managers and trainers need to understand not only external environmental factors influencing the organization, but also these external relationships that affect the organization:

- customers
- vendors
- competitors
- community
- charities
- employees.

In the Real World: Virtual Schools Get a Lift From BellSouth Corporation

One example of a partnership arrangement that illustrates relationships between an organization and its customers, the community, charities, and volunteers is BellSouth Corporation's initiative to provide online instruction in technical and other skills to needy students throughout the southeastern United States with support from a $20 million grant from the BellSouth Foundation.

BellSouth's "20/20 Vision for Education" initiative supports state-led virtual schools and technology-based learning and taps a network of volunteers to provide tutoring and other support. Partners include the Carver School of Technology, part of the Atlanta Public School System's New Schools of Carver, which is serving as a pilot site. In addition, the National Governors Association is helping to promote online learning among high schools as a viable tool to close the achievement gap and improve graduation rates.

In addition to funding seats for Carver students to take virtual courses, BellSouth plans to engage volunteers in technology-based learning programs, such as job shadowing, Project: Connect, e-tutoring, and e-mentoring.

✓ Chapter 14 Knowledge Check

1. New legislation and a partisan climate are examples of which of the following external environmental factors that may influence an organization?

    __ **A.** Global

    __ **B.** Political

    __ **C.** Sociological

    __ **D.** Economic

2. Which of the following analyses can help WLP professionals scan the environment and analyze current and future trends and forces?

    __ **A.** SWOT

    __ **B.** Gantt

    __ **C.** Performance

    __ **D.** Forcefield

3. A geopolitical scan is an inventory of the political, economic, sociological, cultural, global, technological, and employment forces that influence the way an organization functions.

    __ **A.** True

    __ **B.** False

4. Worker skills, corporate responsibilities and ethics, population shifts, immigration, migration, age, and gender are examples of which of the following external environmental factors that may influence an organization?

    __ **A.** Cultural

    __ **B.** Political

    __ **C.** Sociological

    __ **D.** Economic

5. As a result of the last U.S. presidential election, a training director is anticipating the need to increase the amount of OSHA compliance training. Which external environmental factor is this director adjusting to?

    __ **A.** Economic

    __ **B.** Political

    __ **C.** Employment

    __ **D.** Sociological

6. With the advent of automated project management software, clients are starting to expect weekly PERT and Gantt chart updates. Because of these new expectations, a consulting firm needed to change its project management process. Which external environmental factor is this company adjusting to?

    __ **A.** Economic

    __ **B.** Technological

    __ **C.** Global

    __ **D.** Sociological

---

7. Which of the following is an example of an external relationship that affects an organization?

    __ **A.** Customers

    __ **B.** Politcal

    __ **C.** Sociological

    __ **D.** Economic

References

Van Tiem, D., and J. Rosenzweig. (2005). "Performance Excellence Through Partnering." *Infoline* No. 250504.

Verardo, D. (1997). "Managing the Strategic Planning Process." *Infoline* No. 259710.

15
Legal, Regulatory, and Ethical Requirements

Workplace learning and performance (WLP) professionals must be aware of legislative initiatives that affect an organization's strategic vision and employees. One important law, for example, is copyright protection. Using a work protected by copyright for training purposes requires permission from the copyright owner. Knowledge of specific laws or regulations established by a jurisdiction isn't the focus of this chapter, however. The focus is on understanding how laws and regulations may affect design, delivery, and measurement of a learning or performance initiative, which is required for all WLP professionals.

An example of how laws and regulations affect the learning function concerns a creative approach to unleashing the human potential of managers and executives in the form of outdoor experiential or nontraditional training—wilderness treks, offshore sailing jaunts, and other forms of individual or group-survival experiences. These approaches have potentially legal implications, including constitutional issues of religious freedom and privacy, intentional infliction of emotional distress, wrongful discharge, and stress-related claims requiring workers' compensation. For example, a required weekend wilderness excursion for all senior managers may interfere with routine religious activities.

Learning Objectives:

- ☑ Discuss employment law and regulatory requirements regarding licensing and certifications.
- ☑ List two implications of civil rights law on training design.
- ☑ Describe where WLP professionals will find current legislation regarding workplace safety.
- ☑ Describe two considerations regarding securities and financial reporting laws.
- ☑ Discuss the legal implications for information technology (IT) compliance.
- ☑ Discuss the implications of providing training in an organization with a labor union.
- ☑ Discuss the laws related to intellectual property when reproducing material for training.
- ☑ Identify several types of documentation that may be required of a WLP manager and how each should be handled.
- ☑ List four sources of ethical standards governing WLP professionals.

Employment Law and Regulatory Requirements

Regulations of the U.S. *Equal Employment Opportunity Commission (EEOC)* govern hiring, promoting, and discharging of employees. These regulations also cover training situations. The EEOC's Uniform Guidelines on Employee Selection Procedures "apply to tests and other selection procedures which are used as a basis for any employment decision . . . hiring, promotion, demotion. . . . Other selection decisions, such as selection for training or transfer, may be considered employment decisions if they lead to any of the decisions listed above" (29 Code Federal Regulations, Section 1607.2, Ch. XIV, p. 219).

This area of federal law may be the most unfamiliar to WLP professionals. The important legal issues for the human resources (HR) and training function involves lawful selection of people to participate in training and development programs. These situations are practical examples of this issue:

- requiring training before job entry

- selecting employees to attend internal and external programs

- using measures in training as measures of job performance and retention

- assigning jobs based on performance in the training program.

The employer bears the burden of proof to demonstrate that a requirement for employment is related to job performance. Although this principle has eroded somewhat, federal courts still evaluate any job requirement for job relatedness throughout the HR management and development cycle.

A potential legal problem occurs whenever a measure used for a significant employment decision, such as selection for a training program, is discriminatory. The question decided by federal courts is to what extent such a procedure has an "adverse impact on the hiring, promotion, or other employment or membership opportunities of members of any race, sex, or ethnic groups will be considered to be discriminatory . . . unless the procedure has been validated" (29 Code of Federal Regulations, Section 1607.3).

In the context of HR development, a decision to select someone for a training program is a test. For example, an interview to determine eligibility for a training opportunity is just as much a test under the law as the requirement to pass a pencil-and-paper assessment of verbal fluency for entry into an organizationally sponsored program.

Organizations may have an occasion to use testing in the training arena to support other organizational decisions. For example, the selection of employees may be based on criteria (posttest scores) generated from the training environment. One legal question that needs to be addressed is to what extent pre-employment tests are based on successful completion of the program, or whether some other criterion, such as job performance, should be required by test developers.

Glossary of Legal Terms

Thse are some legal terms that WLP professionals may encounter in their work:

Cause of action is a legal claim that is the basis for a lawsuit.

Class action is a lawsuit brought on behalf of many people, all of whom are asserting a common legal claim against a defendant.

Common law is a system of laws originating in England that was based on court decisions and on customs and usages instead of on formal written laws—essentially, these laws are based on common practice that have been upheld in court but have never been legislated.

Copyright refers to legal protection provided for authors of "original works of authorship" that are fixed in a tangible form of expression, including literary, dramatic, musical, artistic, and certain other intellectual properties.

Criminal negligence is negligence that incurs criminal liability and is based on reckless and careless acts resulting in injury or death.

Defendant is the person, institution, or organization being sued by a plaintiff.

Deposition is the verbal questioning of a witness before a trial to discover evidence.

Discovery is the pretrial process of uncovering evidence.

Due process is a constitutional requirement that state and federal governments conduct themselves fairly under the law and avoid arbitrary behavior.

Indictment is a formal charge of a grand jury resulting in a criminal defendant standing trial.

Interrogatories are a series of pretrial questions drawn up for the purpose of determining from witnesses or parties to the case who may have information about the case.

Jurisdiction is the authority of a court to act, either over a person or on a particular cause of action.

Negligence is nonintentional or intentional careless behavior that leads to an injury.

Plaintiff is one who files a lawsuit against a defendant in court.

Proximate cause is the direct or immediate cause, without which an injury would not have occurred, that's sufficient to support an action of negligence.

Statutory law is a body of law created by acts of state and federal legislatures.

Tort is a civil wrong, such as negligence, that may be brought by a plaintiff against a defendant for damages or injunctive relief in a civil court.

For regulatory requirements, many industries require that employees hold appropriate licenses and certifications. Training managers may be responsible for offering courses for licensing and certifications and maintaining a database that tracks all employees, their licensing status, and compliance with any ongoing training and licensing renewals.

Civil Rights

Civil rights legislation related to multilingual participants or those with disabilities has implications to consider during training design. The most recent federal legislation to affect employers is the Americans With Disabilities Act (ADA) of 1990. This act prohibits discrimination in employment, public services, transportation, public accommodations, and telecommunications services against people with disabilities. All aspects of employment are covered, including the application and selection process, on-the-job training, advancement in wages, benefits, and employer-sponsored social activities.

To be considered qualified for a position, a disabled job applicant or employee must be able to perform the essential functions of the job. Employers must reasonably accommodate known mental illness or physical disabilities unless they can demonstrate undue hardship. The ADA does not guarantee people with disabilities the right to a job to which they apply. Employers remain free to make decisions based on the skills or knowledge necessary for the job. An employer is not required to give preference to an applicant with a disability over an applicant without a disability.

With regard to the ADA and training implications, employers must ensure that employees with disabilities have reasonable accommodations that enable them to perform the essential functions of their jobs. Examples include offering auxiliary aids, such as interpreters, magnifying glasses to aid reading, taped text for those who are visually impaired, and instructional material with oversized lettering. These aids should be considered when designing classroom training and e-learning.

Workplace Safety

During the 1960s, concern was raised about safety in the workplace, and in 1970 the U.S. Congress passed the Occupational Safety and Health Act (OSHA). Under OSHA, an employer has a general duty to "furnish to each of his employees employment and a place of employment which is free from recognized hazards that are causing or are likely to cause death or serious harm to his employees . . . " (Sample 1993).

Because this general-duty requirement was so vague, the U.S. Congress intended that the Secretary of Labor promulgate specific safety standards for each industry so that employees would know what to expect. These standards have several implications for trainers and managers of human resource development programs. For example, according to a 1978 U.S. Appeals Court decision, the general duty clause "includes training of employees as to the dangers and supervision of the work site" (*General Dynamics v. OSHARC* 1978; Sample 1993).

Areas of potential liability for technical trainers and their organizations include

- injury to the person being trained, customers, or the general public

- injury from an unsafe training facility or equipment

- failure to train an employee who depends on the training.

Training Implications for Multiple Languages

For classroom-based training and e-learning, intercultural communication and multiple languages can cause barriers to training transfer. For instructor-led and classroom training, training managers may need to provide instruction and training materials in multiple languages to aid in learning transfer. These are some considerations:

Accent and linguistics: An accent is the way a person pronounces, enumerates, and articulates words. Trainers and managers need to consider the trainer and target audience and try to provide an instructor who speaks the same language and has a similar accent or dialect as the target audience.

Gross translation errors: When translating training materials into multiple languages, gross translation errors are relatively frequent and usually easy to detect and correct. The General Motors slogan "Body by Fisher," for example, was once translated as "Corpse by Fisher." The possibility of conflict arises when one party attributes the mistranslation to disrespect for the receiving culture.

Nuance errors: When two parties don't have similar command of a language, mild distinctions between meanings can lead to misunderstandings. The nuances between "misunderstand" and "misinterpret," for example, affect a person's ability to understand.

Securities and Financial Reporting

Since 1973, the Financial Accounting Standards Board has been the designated organization in the private sector for establishing standards of financial accounting and reporting. Those standards govern the preparation of financial reports and are officially recognized by the Securities and Exchange Commission (SEC). Accounting standards are essential to the economy's efficient functioning because decisions about the allocation of resources rely heavily on credible, concise, and understandable financial information. Financial information about the operations and financial position of entities is also used by the public in making other kinds of decisions.

The SEC has statutory authority to establish financial accounting and reporting standards for publicly held companies under the Securities Exchange Act of 1934. Throughout its history, however, the SEC's policy has been to rely on the private sector for this function to the extent that the private sector demonstrates the ability to fulfill the responsibility in the public interest.

In the Real World: OSHA General-Duty Requirements Case

OSHA cited the shipbuilding division of General Dynamics Corporation for failing to give adequate instructions to employees who were tack-welding vertical standing steel plates. According to the case facts, employees were involved in tack-welding a 26-by-6-foot vertically standing steel plate that weighed 3,500 pounds. They were welding the plate to another large, horizontal plate resting on a platform. The vertical plates were supported by two pairs of 80-pound braced monuments bolted on each side of the plate. One side of the steel plate had been tack-welded by an earlier shift. Shortly after the second shift began, a beginning shipfitter started work, and three of the braced monuments were removed. When the shipfitter removed the fourth brace to align the work, the 3,500-pound plate collapsed, killing an employee.

General Dynamics argued that it provided safety instruction on the use of the monuments and that it had a safety manual with instructions for shipfitters. Evidence determined that experienced employees as well as the beginning shipfitter didn't know when a vertically standing steel place could be considered securely welded and didn't know when it was safe to remove the monuments. Although the beginning shipfitter had been instructed once, it was not adequate in view of the seriousness of the hazard, and the safety manual didn't have proper explanations for securing the plates or procedures for removing the monuments.

Source: Adapted from Sample (1993).

Businesses report information in the form of four financial statements issued periodically. Generally Accepted Accounting Principles require four primary financial statements:

1. balance sheet
2. income statement
3. statement of cash flows
4. statement of owner's equity.

The training manager may be required to ensure that employees in finance and accounting departments have the training needed to ensure that the organization is in compliance with how they prepare and publish financial statements.

The Sarbanes-Oxley Act of 2002 is important legislation affecting corporate governance, financial disclosure, and the practice of public accounting since the U.S. Securities laws of the 1930s. Sparked by several high-profile securities and accounting scandals, such as Enron, the act was passed to protect investors from fraudulent accounting activities by improving the accuracy and reliability of corporate disclosures. This act includes 11 titles, but most organizations focus on those sections concerned with internal controls to ensure accurate financial reporting—and organizations must document these controls.

This legislation, while imposing deadlines for large and small companies, requires publicly listed companies to prove that their internal controls are sufficient. To do so, organizations must ensure that employees understand specific processes and procedures—which must be documented and achieved through formal training.

IT Compliance

IT organizations need to identify, develop, implement, and maintain emerging and rapidly changing information technologies. These organizations may focus on technologies to improve the usability, reliability, and security of computers and computer networks for work and home. For all systems and architecture to work together, national IT standards have been established. To help IT departments stay ahead of the IT curve and use new technologies in the organization, training managers must provide access to courses and programs for the IT group to be in compliance with new technologies and earn any required certifications.

Union Relations

Union activity between the 1930s and the mid-1950s provided the impetus for the development and passage of two acts that affect training and development. The National Labor Relations Act of 1947, also referred to as the Wagner Act, prohibits discrimination against union employees with respect to terms and conditions of employment, including apprenticeships and training programs. The National Labor Relations Board considers training to be a condition of employment and a mandatory subject for collective bargaining. The Labor-Management Relations Act, also known as the Taft-Hartley Act, prevents unions from discriminating for any reason except payment of dues and assessments. The act also permits noncoercive employer free speech, which may affect trainers. For example, if a company president supports a particular political party, it could be assumed that employees support that party. In training, instructors should use no examples, case studies, or role plays that infringe on a person's personal philosophy or belief system.

Organizations with labor unions mean additional considerations for the training function. As noted by Howard (1996), "Led by the Congress of Industrial Organizations, labor reforms of the 1930s reorganized many unions on an industry-wide basis, mixing skilled and unskilled workers in the same union. This arrangement strengthened the unions' bargaining power. Distinctions regarding the mastery of skills were dealt with through contract language that defined job classifications and wages. Unions retain a leading role in defining skill levels associated with job titles or craft titles."

Training organizations and the HR department work with the local union to define the type of training that should be provided. For example, providing safety training to meet OSHA guidelines is the responsibility of the training department. The training department must also maintain the records of those who have completed all required training successfully. Because of on-the-job training required to master necessary trades and skills, unions are active in creating, implementing, and monitoring apprenticeship programs in the United States. As Howard (1996) points out, the craft orientation of many unions provides a natural vehicle for transmission of skills related to the trade. Unions also foster pride and accomplishment associated with the mastery of skill levels in a certain trade. Many unions have established their own formal or informal apprenticeship programs to protect the integrity of the craft and to bargain effectively for union members. In states with joint apprenticeship councils, unions are a major player in the process. Labor organizations continue to protect the integrity of the journey-level status within their trade.

Intellectual Property

Trainers try to use the most recent materials during training events. WLP professionals must set an example that doesn't encourage others to use material requiring previous permission for use. The design and development of training programs likely requires using or incorporating various sources of information, so care must be taken with copyright requirements. Copyright, as defined by the Society for Human Resource Management guidelines (McArdle 1999), is "the exclusive right or privilege of the author or proprietor to print or otherwise multiply, distribute, and vend copies of his/her literary, artistic, or intellectual productions when secured by compliance with the copyright statute." This statute also gives authors the right to prepare derivative works.

The Copyright Act of 1976 stipulates that copyright begins with the creation of the work in a fixed form from which it can be perceived or communicated. The exclusive rights of the author or proprietor are limited by the fair use of copyrighted works in certain circumstances. Whether a use is fair depends on several factors, including the

- *purpose and character of the use*, including whether the use of material is commercial in nature or for nonprofit educational purpose

- *nature* of the copyrighted work

- *amount*, or substantiality, of the portion used in relation to the copyrighted work as a whole

- *effect* on market potential for or value of the copyrighted work.

Copyright law protects the expression of an idea (but not the idea itself) in some tangible form (book, magazine, video, film, microfilm, cassette tape, computer disk, and so forth). Although the exact words in a book may be copyrighted, the ideas in the book are not. The following cannot be copyrighted: ideas, processes, procedures, methods of operation, concepts, principles, or discoveries. However, a tangible description, explanation, or illustration of them may be copyrighted.

Fair use standards may apply to training materials as well. Trainers often make a single copy of a copyrighted material for personal use. Training managers should check with the copyright holder before making multiple copies of copyrighted works.

For anonymous works and works made for hire (such as those prepared by a trainer or other employees at the request of employers), the period of protection lasts for 75 years from the first publication or 100 years from the year of creation, whichever expires first. Employers, rather than the trainer who did the writing, are considered authors of the work and the owners of the copyright. According to the U.S. Copyright

Office, "The use of a copyright notice is no longer required under U.S. law, although it is often beneficial. Because prior law did contain such a requirement, however, the use of notice is still relevant to the copyright status of older works. Use of the notice may be important because it informs the public that the work is protected by copyright, identifies the copyright owner, and shows the year of first publication. The use of the copyright notice is the responsibility of the copyright owner and does not require advance permission from, or registration with, the Copyright Office" (U.S. Copyright Office 2006).

Copyright registration is a legal formality intended to make a public record of the basic facts of a particular copyright. However, registration is not a condition of copyright protection. Even though registration is not a requirement for protection, the copyright law provides several inducements or advantages to encourage copyright owners to make registration. Advantages of registration include a public record of the copyright claim, evidence of validity of copyright claim, and availability of statutory damages and attorney's fees in court actions.

A copyright is secured immediately and automatically when the work is created, and a work is created when it's fixed in some form of a tangible expression (computer disk, print copy, and so forth). Registering the work with the U.S. Copyright Office provides legal protection and redress in state and federal courts.

A copyright holder has these exclusive rights:

- the right to reproduce the copyrighted work

- the right to prepare derivative works (adaptation) based on the copyrighted work

- the right to distribute copies of the copyrighted work to the public by sale or other transfer of ownership or by rental, lease, or lending

- the right to perform the copyrighted work publicly, in the case of motion pictures or other audiovisual works

- the right to display the copyrighted work publicly, in the case of audiovisual work.

Exclusive rights are qualified by the fair use privilege. This privilege allows others to use copyrighted material in a reasonable manner without consent. Although legal guidelines exist, fair use is a tricky legal concept to understand. An author is free to copy from a protected work for purposes of criticism, news reporting, teaching, or research so long as the value of the copyrighted work isn't diminished for the author. Proper citations should always be used to avoid passing the work off as original (known as plagiarism). The best practice is to obtain written consent from the copyright holder to use the materials, even for an educational program. However, protection is available to use these materials in the training context; despite this fact, being sure all citations or other attribution to the copyrighted work are included is prudent.

Intellectual property issues have also been controversial in the field due in large part to the Internet. WLP professionals should be aware of digital copyright considerations:

- Copyrights protect the expression of an idea, a concept, or a thought in tangible form, so WLP professionals must be sure to attribute electronic text appropriately and get permission to use copyrighted material.

- Limited exceptions to the permission rule are possible under the fair use doctrine, which includes reproducing portions of original works for criticism or comment, news reporting, teaching and scholarship, and research. Additional caveats include whether the use will generate profit or depreciate the value of the copyrighted work.

- WLP professionals should watch for new legislation—the Technology Education and Copyright Harmonization Act of 2001—that would free educators to use copyrighted materials in distance learning programs. Current copyright law enables schools to avoid paying royalties for copyrighted materials used in live instruction, but the same use in e-learning courses requires a license.

A work that has fallen into the public domain is available for use without permission from the copyright owner or payment to that person. A work is considered public domain if it meets one of the following requirements:

- It was published before January 1, 1978, without notice of copyright.

- The period of copyright protection has expired.

- It was produced for the U.S. government by its officers or employees as part of their official duties.

Until recently, copyrights had little to do with trainers' daily work. Intellectual property was easy to protect. However, with the advent of the Internet, any computer user can easily copy, distribute, or publish almost anything on the Internet. This technology threatens to make copyright and intellectual property safeguards obsolete. However, messages or articles passed on a Usenet newsgroup or via email are automatically copyrighted by the authors.

Corporate Policies and Procedures

Organizations also have their own internal policies and procedures to document guidelines and procedures and to ensure compliance. Some sources of information and strategies training organizations can use to help ensure that the workforce has knowledge of corporate policies and procedures include

- HR strategy white papers

- status reports for managers on the development of their staff and compliance with completing mandatory courses

- learning plan tracking

- improved human and organizational performance

- education of senior management on WLP principles

- professional service agreements
- return-on-investment data.

Ethical Standards

Because of rapidly changing technology, competition, and business environments, many training departments have instituted just-in-time training. Training managers want to schedule education classes on short notice, triggered by specific enrollment minimums. Training departments, if they go to outside vendors, are getting better at demanding precise customization for a specific target population. Managers know it's a buyers' market—and they demand top quality at rock-bottom prices. With so many vendors pursuing the same companies in this business environment, the opportunity for unethical practices has increased on both sides of the business transaction.

The Harvard Business School offered the first course in business ethics in 1915. Since the mid-1980s, many other business schools have offered courses in business ethics. These courses have become quite popular in most business school curriculums; however, many academic and business managers admit in private that the topic is too esoteric to influence everyday business decisions much. Too often, business ethics concerns itself with theorizing.

If business ethics is to have a significant influence, ethical business practices require acting with an awareness of the need to comply with the business community's rules, customs, and expectations. They also include the business policies of organizations involved in the transaction. In addition, ethical training and development practices must involve the effects of products, services, or trainer's actions on an organization's employees.

Professional Association Guidelines and Codes of Conduct

Training professionals need to focus on the basic values that help lead people to more consistently ethical behaviors. Some organizations have developed guidelines and codes of conduct that they want their managers and employees to espouse. The following sections present samples of ethical codes.

The Academy of Professional Consultants and Advisors' Code of Professional Ethics

The Academy of Professional Consultants and Advisors (APCA) has developed a code for its members. All professional members of the APCA agree to adhere to its Code of Professional Ethics:

- Maintain a wholly professional attitude and behavior toward clients, other professionals, employees, and the public at large.

- Maintain and advance the standards of professional practice, and encourage others to understand the purposes and standards of practice.

- Avoid taking advantage (for personal or financial gain) of information obtained through professional assignments and relationships.

- Avoid improprieties or the appearance of improprieties.

- Avoid marketing, advertising, or other professional activities that may use language that would be misleading, unprofessional, or damaging to the profession.

- Avoid conflicts of interest in service to clients and maintain confidentiality with respect to all services provided.

- Provide services only within the scope of professional competence and on the basis of demonstrated need, objectivity, and independence.

- Communicate fees or the basis of fee determination in advance of the provision of services, and communicate the objectives to be obtained from the services prior to, or in the very early stages of, an engagement.

- Do not disclose proprietary data or information obtained while serving a client to others or make use of such data or information in the service of another client without the permission of the rightful owner of such data and information.

- Maintain a position of professional independence in servicing clients, and inform clients of any biases or interest that might impair independence or objectivity.

American Society for Training & Development National Code of Ethics

The American Society for Training and Development (ASTD) developed a national code of ethics for its members that offers guidance for trainers to be self-managed WLP professionals. Clients and employers should expect the highest possible standards of personal integrity, professional competence, sound judgment, and discretion from ASTD members. Developed by the profession for the profession, the ASTD Code of Ethics is the public declaration of WLP professionals' obligations to themselves, their profession, and society. It states that its members strive to

- recognize the rights and dignities of each individual

- develop human potential

- provide their employers, clients, and learners with the highest level of quality education, training, and development

- comply with all copyright laws and the laws and regulations governing their position

- keep informed of pertinent knowledge and competence in the WLP field

- maintain confidentiality and integrity in the practice of their profession

- support their peers and avoid conduct that impedes practicing their profession

- conduct themselves in an ethical and honest manner

- improve the public understanding of WLP

- fairly and accurately represent their WLP credentials, qualifications, experience, and abilities

- contribute to the continuing growth of the profession.

Industry Standards

The following are general standards for the WLP industry. In addition, buyers and sellers should develop practices and guidelines to fit the unique needs of their professional relationships.

The behaviors in the relationship between buyers and sellers of training and educational services or products are subdivided into three basic activities: contracting, developing or delivering, and maintaining. Current standards, practices, and guidelines related to these behaviors have evolved from the industry's professional activities. Additional changes are anticipated in the future. The practices promote the concept of business self-regulation through the efforts of the Better Business Bureau.

Standards are defined as specific rules (requirements and criteria) that are widely accepted by training experts. Practices include the everyday behaviors of operational methods (application and execution) that are followed consistently throughout the contemporary WLP industry. Guidelines are generally accepted concepts, opinions, or theories that are often, but not always, followed by members of the WLP community.

Buyers include presidents or owners, directors, executives, managers, and trainers. Sellers are vendors, consultants, trainers, salespeople or marketers, developers or designers, and those responsible for developing and delivering training or educational programs to industry.

Conciliation is the involvement of a neutral third party to help disputants communicate by letter or phone and work out a solution to a problem. Mediation is a structured process guided by a neutral third party with specific steps that are followed to clarify issues and discuss options and solutions. Arbitration is a process in which two or more people agree to let an impartial person or panel decide their dispute.

Self-Governing Behaviors

To what extent do training managers' personal values establish the basis for their business decisions and strategies? WLP professionals need to focus on the basic values that help lead people to more consistent ethical behaviors. According to the American Bar Association and the American Arbitration Association, those basic values include

- *honesty:* a personal, objective, and constant commitment to being a witness to truth

- *fairness:* impartiality in all business relationships, as evidenced by respecting the diversity of others in an equal and just manner

- *lawfulness:* observance of both the letter and spirit of the laws governing commerce, individual rights in the workplace, and expectations of customers

- *compassion:* response to the human needs of others in a personal and moral manner that recognizes the dignity of human life

- *respect:* recognition that all human beings require an understanding of their thinking, the activities in their personal lives, and the individual beliefs that make them unique

- *loyalty:* a sense of personal trust between people, among groups of employees, between employer and worker, or between a business and its clients

- *dependability:* consistent personal behavior that meets or exceeds the expectations of all concerned parties.

✓ Chapter 15 Knowledge Check

1. **According to EEOC laws, HR professionals and training managers need to be careful about the selection of someone for a training program because these criteria and selection process are considered a test.**

   __ **A.** True

   __ **B.** False

2. **Important legal issues for HR and the training function involving lawful selection of people to participate in WLP programs include all the following *except***

   __ **A.** Requiring training before job entry

   __ **B.** Using measures in training as measures of job performance and retention

   __ **C.** Selecting employees to attend internal and external programs

   __ **D.** Assigning job based on performance in previous job roles

3. **An outdoor experiential team-building training program that one vendor offers includes rigorous adventure activities, such as whitewater rafting. One employee refuses to attend because the program takes place on a Saturday, which she observes as a religious holiday. If the organization insists that she attend or face termination, which of the following laws is in violation?**

   __ **A.** ADA

   __ **B.** OSHA

   __ **C.** Civil rights

   __ **D.** Intellectual property

4. **Which of the following is *not* an example of a reasonable accommodation that the training function must provide for people with disabilities?**

   __ **A.** Magnifying glasses

   __ **B.** Larger text materials

   __ **C.** Customized one-on-one training

   __ **D.** Interpreters

5. **An instructional designer needs to include information on current legislation regarding fork lift safety in her training class. Which of the following is the official source charged with providing specific safety standards?**

   __ **A.** National Safety Council

   __ **B.** Secretary of Labor

   __ **C.** Small Business Association

   __ **D.** National Labor Relations Board

6. **The Sarbanes-Oxley Act of 2002 affects which of the following types of legislation?**

   __ **A.** EEOC

   __ **B.** OSHA

   __ **C.** Civil rights

   __ **D.** Security and financial reporting

7. **To comply with national IT standards, IT training managers must provide access to courses and programs for the IT group.**

   __ **A.** True

   __ **B.** False

8. **A training department is responsible for training a large number of unionized employees. How will unions most likely affect the training provided to employees?**

   __ **A.** Unions approve the content of the training.

   __ **B.** Unions set the number of required training hours.

   __ **C.** Unions help define the skill levels associated with job titles.

   __ **D.** Unions select which employees will participate in the training.

9. **Which of the following is *not* one of the exclusive rights of copyright holders?**

   __ **A.** To reproduce the copyrighted work

   __ **B.** To perform the copyrighted work publicly

   __ **C.** To copyright the initial idea that the copyrighted work was derived from

   __ **D.** To prepare derivative works based on the copyrighted work

10. **A WLP professional needs to distribute copies but is not sure the fair use doctrine applies. Then, the WLP professional notices that the copyright date is five years old; therefore, the copyright privileges no longer apply to the published information.**

    __ **A.** True

    __ **B.** False

11. **Which of the following is *not* an example of corporate policy and procedure documentation?**

    __ **A.** HR strategy white papers

    __ **B.** Status reports and compliance with completion of mandatory courses

    __ **C.** Intellectual property laws

    __ **D.** ROI data

12. **Ethical standards for WLP professionals include professional association guidelines; industry standards; codes of conduct; and self-governing behaviors, including honesty, integrity, respect, and accountability.**

    __ **A.** True

    __ **B.** False

References

Abernathy, D.J. (August 2001). "Digital Copyrights and Wrongs." *T&D* , pp. 27–30.

Eyers, P.S. (1996). "Training and the Law." *The ASTD Training and Development Handbook* (4th edition), R.L. Craig, editor. New York: McGraw-Hill.

Gordon, E.E., and J.E. Baumhart. (1995). "Ethics for Training and Development." *Infoline* No. 259515. (Out of print.)

Howard, A.H. (1996). "Apprenticeship." *The ASTD Training and Development Handbook* (4th edition), R.L. Craig, editor. New York: McGraw-Hill.

Johnson, G. (October 2004). "The Perfect Storm." *Training*, pp. 38–49.

Johnson, J. (2004). "Ethics for Trainers." *Infoline* No. 250406.

Lectric Law Library. "Lexicon on Common Law." www.lectlaw.com/def/c070.htm.

McArdle, G.E. (1999). *Training Design and Delivery*. Alexandria, VA: ASTD Press.

Sample, J. (1993). "Legal Liability & HRD: Implications for Trainers." *Infoline* No. 259309. (Out of print.)

U.S. Copyright Office. (2006). "About Copyright." www.copyright.gov/circs/circ1.html.

Appendix A
Glossary

ADDIE is an instructional systems development model composed of five phases:

1. **Analysis** is the process of gathering data to identify specific needs—the who, what, where, when, and why of the design process.

2. **Design** is the planning stage.

3. **Development** is the phase in which training materials and content are selected and developed based on learning objectives.

4. **Implementation** occurs when the course is delivered, whether in person or electronically.

5. **Evaluation** is the ongoing process of developing and improving instructional materials based on feedback received during and after implementation.

Andragogy (from Greek meaning "adult learning") is the adult learning theory popularized by Malcolm Knowles, based on five key principles that influence how adults learn: self-concept, previous experience, readiness to learn, orientation to learning, and motivation to learn.

Asynchronous Training or Learning refers to a scenario that doesn't require the trainer and the learner to participate simultaneously, for example, email and threaded discussions.

Authoring Tools are special software programs (including Macromedia Authorware) that allow a content expert to interact with the computer in everyday language to help develop CBT courseware.

Codec (short for coder/decoder) is a device used for video teleconferencing. A camera's video signal is fed to an electronic box called a codec. The codec converts the audio-visual signals into digital information. The information is then sent, over high-capacity phone lines, to remote sites. After remote sites have received the digital information, the codec at each site converts the digital signal back to a signal that can be displayed on a television monitor.

Collaborative Learning is an instructional approach in which learners and instructors share the responsibility for learning and work together to determine how the session should progress.

Collaborative Learning Software, including email, computer networks, whiteboards, bulletin board systems, chat rooms, and online presentation tools, offers a way to familiarize learners with new expectations and experiences. These technologies play an important role in the expansion of e-learning and in collaborating on projects, sharing information, and communicating.

Computer-Based Training (CBT) encompasses the use of computers in both instruction and management of the training and learning process. Computer-assisted instruction and computer-managed instruction are included under the term *CBT.*

Distance Learning is an educational situation in which the instructor and students are separated by time, location, or both. Education or training courses are delivered to remote locations via synchronous or asynchronous training.

E-Learning is a term covering a wide set of applications and processes, such as web-based learning, computer-based learning, virtual classrooms, and digital collaboration. Delivery of content may be via the Internet, an intranet/extranet (LAN/WAN), audiotapes and videotapes, satellite broadcasts, interactive television, CD-ROMs, and more.

Electronic Performance Support System (EPSS) is a software program that provides just-in-time, on-demand information, guidance, examples, and step-by-step dialog boxes to improve job performance without the need for training or coaching by other people.

Equal Employment Opportunity Commission (EEOC) creates regulations that govern hiring, promoting, and discharging employees. These regulations also cover training situations.

Evaluation of training is a systematic method for gathering information about the effectiveness and effect of training programs. Results of the measurements can be used to improve the offering, determine whether the learning objectives have been achieved, and assess the value of the training to the organization.

Gantt Chart graphically displays the time relationships of the project's steps and key checkpoints or deliverable dates, known as milestones.

Human Resource Development (HRD) is the term coined by Leonard Nadler to describe the organized learning experiences of training, education, and development offered by employers within a specific timeframe to improve employee performance or personal growth. It's also another name for the field sometimes called training or training and development.

Instructional Designer is a person who applies a systematic methodology based on instructional theory to create learning content.

Instructional System is the combination of inputs, such as subject matter and resources, and outputs, such as curriculum and materials, to build a training course.

Instructional Systems Development (ISD) is a systems approach to analyzing, designing, developing, implementing, and evaluating any instructional experience based on the belief that training is most effective when it gives learners a clear statement of what they must be able to do as a result of training and how their performance will be evaluated. The program is designed to teach skills through hands-on practice or performance-based instruction.

Intranet is a network of computers that's accessible only to authorized users. Intranets use the same software and technology that works on the Internet.

Job Aids provide guidance or assistance, either audio or visual, to job performers about when to carry out tasks and steps, thereby reducing the amount of recall that's needed and minimizing error. Good candidates for job aids are usually tasks performed with relatively low frequency, highly complex tasks, tasks likely to change in the future, and tasks that include a high probability of error.

Knowledge Exchanges, also known as knowledge exchange networks, enable different groups in an organization to share documents and information on products to create lists of links in simple web pages and to discuss issues of mutual interest.

KSA is an abbreviation that has two definitions: 1. Knowledge (cognitive), skills (psychomotor), and attitudes (affective) are the three objective domains of learning defined by Benjamin Bloom's taxonomy in the 1950s. 2. Knowledge, skills, and ability are commonly referred to as KSAs and used by federal and private hiring agencies to determine the attributes or qualities an employee possesses for a job.

Learning Content Management System (LCMS) combines the most essential pieces of the learning puzzle—namely, courses and learning materials. LCMSs package content for print, CD-ROM, or electronic publication, and most are capable of importing prepackaged content from other learning content development tools, such as Microsoft Word and Macromedia Dreamweaver.

Learning Information System is a tool that benefits the training manager on several levels: program administration and design and delivery of training.

Learning Management System (LMS) consists of software that automates the administration of training. The LMS registers users, tracks courses in a catalog, records data from learners, and provides reports to management. An LMS typically is designed to handle courses by multiple publishers and providers.

Learning Objects are self-contained chunks of instructional material used in LCMSs. They typically include three components: a performance goal, the necessary learning content to reach that goal, and some form of evaluation to measure whether or not the goal was achieved.

Learning Style describes an individual's approach to learning that involves the way he or she behaves, feels, and processes information.

Multisensory Learning engages the learner and increases retention. Audio and video can often convey feelings and subtle contexts of learning more effectively than other tools.

Objective is a target or purpose that, when combined with other objectives, leads to a goal.

Outsourcing Training refers to using resources or products external to an organization to meet an organization's learning requirements.

Program Evaluation Review Technique (PERT) Chart is a diagramming technique that enables project managers to estimate a range of task durations by estimating the optimistic, pessimistic, and most likely durations for each task.

Project Life Cycle is everything that happens from the beginning to the end of the project.

Project Management is the planning, organizing, directing, and controlling of resources for a finite period of time to complete specific goals and objectives.

Project Scope is what will or won't be done on the project. Project scope management includes the processes needed to complete all required work (and only the required work) so that the project is completed successfully.

Scope Creep refers to the work or deliverables that are added to a project but were neither part of the project requirements nor added through a formal requirement change.

Server is the machine where e-learning instruction is hosted.

Simulation is an exercise with a simplified form of a real-life situation so that participants can practice making decisions and analyze results of those decisions.

Subject Matter Expert (SME) is a person who has extensive knowledge and skills in a particular subject area.

Synchronous Training refers to a scenario that involves the trainer and the trainee participating at the same time. It often refers to electronic or web-based training.

Training Manager is primarily responsible for identifying training needs, developing a strategy to meet target audience needs, and securing resources to fill those needs.

Training Needs Assessment is the process of collecting and synthesizing data to identify how training can help an organization reach its goals.

Training Objective is a statement of what the instructor hopes to accomplish during the training session.

Virtual Reality (VR) is a computer-based technology that gives learners a realistic, three-dimensional, interactive experience. This powerful tool enhances learning by allowing students to perform skills in a realistic, engaging simulation of a real-life environment.

Vision describes an organization as its members would like it to be, in terms of corporate image, values, employee satisfaction, markets, and products or services.

Web-Based Training (WBT) refers to the delivery of educational content via a web browser over the Internet, a private intranet, or an extranet.

Work Breakdown Structure (WBS) is the primary tool used to begin planning and documenting project deliverables.

WYSIWYG (pronounced "wizzy-wig") means "what you see is what you get." WYSIWYG applications don't always display code; instead they provide a working area where text and graphics are placed on the screen.

Appendix B
Answer Key

Chapter 4

1. Which of the following delivery methods is best for learners with a low level of self-directeness?

D. Classroom instruction

Response D is the correct response because classroom learning requires that learners be present. In addition, it is the job of the training facilitator to ensure that all attendees engage with the material being presented.

2. Which delivery method has the primary advantages of being excellent for teaching rote skills and prerequisite materials, offering flexibility in scheduling, and being capable of quick delivery?

C. E-learning

Response C is correct because e-learning can be repeated as many times as it takes to learn rote skills without the learner having to feel embarrassed if he or she does not succeed at first. Similarly, the learner can prepare for classroom training sessions by using e-learning on his or her own time to brush up on prerequisite materials.

3. A manager of a small company is trying to decide if high-end simulations are an appropriate training option to deliver new product training to salespeople. Which of the following factors makes simulations inappropriate for this company?

C. The training will be updated quarterly.

Response C is correct because simulations or other high-end e-learning content typically require lengthy development timelines and have high development costs. Quarterly updates would be expensive and could probably not be achieved in a sufficient amount of time.

4. With video teleconferencing, the equipment is often the same at both the instructor site and the learner sites, which provides the flexibility for any site in the system to become an instructor site.

A. True

Response A is correct because video teleconferencing provides the capability of two-way transmission of both audio and video signals, which requires that the equipment is the same at both instructor and learner sites.

5. Which of the following is *not* an advantage of a job aid?

B. Excellent for tasks with short reaction time

Response B is correct because tasks with short reaction time require that the performer be able to do what he or she needs to do without taking the time to find a job aid and look up what to do. In other words, the performer needs to know what to do at a moment's notice; this is true in the case of, for example, a pilot reacting to an emergency on a plane.

6. The benefits of audio and video in instruction include enabling multisensory learning.

A. True

Response A is correct because multimedia helps learners retain and understand information. Multimedia stimulates several senses, thereby keeping the learners interested, and appeals to learners with different preferences for taking in information, whether audio, visual, or kinesthetic.

7. A manager is reviewing the reasons for providing employees with an EPSS as a job aid. Of the following scenarios, which one is considered the best reason for using an EPSS?

B. Employees require just-in-time performance assistance.

Response B is correct because for employees that need just-in-time performance assistance EPSS provides on-demand information, guidance, examples, and step-by-step dialog boxes without the need for training or coaching.

8. One of the biggest barriers to implementing technology-based learning is

A. Organizational culture

Response A is correct because no matter how great and streamlined the technologies, if the organizational culture and perceptions of the learners do not accept technology-based learning or perceive that it is inferior to traditional classroom instruction, then nothing will make the learning program a success.

9. Which of the following was created in an effort to minimize or remove technical roadblocks and fosters creation of reuseable learning content as "instructional objects"?

A. SCORM

Response A is correct because SCORM stands for Sharable Content Object Reference Model. SCORM was designed by the Department of Defense to foster creation of reusable learning content as "instructional objects" within a common technical framework consisting of guidelines, specifications, and standards.

10. When selecting a learning technology, the most important consideration in the selection process is

A. Identifying the learning objectives and desired outcomes and selecting the technology to support those goals

Response A is correct because the organizational culture plays the most significant role if e-learning is supported and if technology-based learning will be sustained for future efforts. If sponsors and learners do not believe that technology-based learning solutions are beneficial and preferable to traditional instructional approaches, then the learning programs will likely fail.

11. Which of the following is best defined as a term covering a wide set of applications and processes, such as virtual classrooms, digital collaboration, and so on? Delivery of content may be via the Internet/intranet/extranet (LAN/WAN), audiotape and videotape, satellite broadcast, interactive TV, CD-ROM, and more.

B. E-learning

Response B is correct because e-learning is an umbrella term that refers to anything delivered, enabled, or mediated by electronic technology for the purpose of learning, and it can be delivered through a wide variety of methods.

12. Video teleconferencing allows the instructor to see learners and vice versa.

A.True

Response A is correct because video teleconferencing refers to a two-way transmission of both audio and video signals.

13. Which of the following is best described as an exercise with a simplified form of a real-life situation so that participants can practice making decisions and analyzing results of those decisions?

A. Simulations

Response A is correct because a simulation is a representation of a piece of equipment or a system that enables users to provide inputs and see the system's typical responses. This enables learners to practice doing certain tasks and see the results of what they have done in a safe environment.

14. A WLP professional working in a federal government agency is instructed by his manager that the e-learning content he is researching to purchase from a vendor must be accessible by federal employees with disabilities. The standard that the manager is referencing is

B. Section 508

Response B is correct because Section 508 refers to a standard in the Americans with Disabilities Act that requires that when federal agencies develop, procure, maintain, or use EIT, federal employees with disabilities must have comparable access to and use of information and data as federal employees who have no disabilities, unless an undue burden would be imposed on the agency.

15. Which of the following is defined as a CBT that gives learners a realistic, three-dimensional, interactive experience?

C. VR

Response C is correct because VR is a CBT that allows learners to perform skills in a realistic, engaging simulation of a real-life environment.

16. A WLP professional is creating a blended learning program and wants to leverage collaboration tools to facilitate the learning process and provide informal learning experiences for the target audience outside of formal classroom instruction. All of the following are examples of collaboration software *except*

D. LMSs

Response D is correct because an LMS is a software application that automates administering, tracking, and reporting learning events.

Chapter 5

1. Which of the following systems manages content, such as components that make up a course?

B. LCMS

Response B is correct because an LCMS is a system that creates, stores, assembles, and delivers learning content in the form of learning objects, which are self-contained chunks of self-instructional material.

2. Which of the following systems manages learners, including who's taking what, completion ratios, course progress status, and scheduling?

A. LMS

Response A is correct because an LMS provides access to learning resources and manages the administrative side of learning.

3. Which of the following is *not* a benefit of an LCMS?

D. Integration with HR systems

Response D is correct because an LCMS is not involved with the administrative side of learning (unlike an LMS); an LCMS is used to manage learning content.

4. Which of the following includes email, computer networks, whiteboards, bulletin board systems, chat rooms, and online presentation tools, which can play an important role in the expansion of e-learning and in collaborating on projects, sharing information, and communicating?

D. Collaboration tools

Response D is correct because collaboration tools provide an environment that enables learners to work together electronically, thereby enabling them to collaborate on projects and assist one another's learning.

5. An LMS supports pretesting and adaptive learning.

B. False

Response B is correct because an LMS does not support pretesting and adaptive learning. That is a function of an LCMS.

6. The implementation of learning information systems can cause changes in an organization's management style and roles within the line structure.

A. True

Response A is correct because using learning information systems can cause changes in an organization's management and roles by enabling the organization to align learning initiatives with strategic goals and offer employees courses that can enhance their career paths.

7. An organization's training department is deciding if it should purchase a learning information system. Which of the following is *not* a likely effect of the learning information system adoption?

D. Better able to deal with technology compatibility issues

Response D is correct because integrating existing systems and security issues in an organization may cause compatibility issues rather than solve them.

8. Which of the following is *not* one of the assessments that should be conducted prior to implementing an LMS?

C. Training needs assessment

Response C is correct because implementing an LMS does not require a training needs assessment. Because an LMS does not actually provide learning materials, there is no need to determine whether the organization's employees need any particular training.

9. A training department is collecting requirements for selecting an LCMS. Which of the following is a typical LCMS function?

C. Create test questions

Response C is correct because an LCMS combines the most essential pieces of the learning puzzle, including creating and administering tests.

Chapter 6

1. Before making a decision to purchase printed participant materials, the training director always insists on checking if a table of contents, an index, and a glossary are included. Why is checking these components important when reviewing printed training materials?

B. Facilitates learning after training

Response B is correct because elements like tables of contents, indexes, and glossaries help learners to go back to their participant materials after they have received training to increase retention and improve their ability to apply what they have learned.

2. All of the following are key elements to consider when reviewing off-the-shelf e-learning courseware *except*

C. Revision schedules

Response C is correct because revision schedules are unnecessary to consider for off-the-shelf e-learning courseware, which is developed and purchased once and isn't revised throughout the course of its life.

3. Many considerations are different when evaluating e-learning versus web-based training materials.

B. False

Response B is correct because many considerations are the same for evaluating e-learning and for evaluating web-based training. E-learning and web-based training are similar to any training method in that it doesn't provide a good ROI unless end users are successful at performing the learning objectives and the program achieves its overall goal of increased performance.

4. Outsourcing usually refers to deciding whether to use external products and resources to meet business needs.

A. True

Response A is correct because outsourcing involves acquiring specialized expertise that an organization does not want to staff full time or to get external support for employees who lack certain skill sets.

5. An organization needs to develop a training program to support a new product launch and salesforce training. Which of the following is the best benefit of developing materials and training programs in-house?

B. Designers and developers have firsthand knowledge of the company, culture, mission, and goals.

Response B is correct because in-house designers and developers understand the culture of the organization, which enables them to create learning that fits the culture and that appeals to the organization's learners.

6. A key benefit of outsourcing includes identifying how to best use internal resources and leverage external resources.

A. True

Response A is correct because outsourcing requires planning to ensure that the organization selects and carries out the best outsourcing solution. The first step in doing this is determining the need, which involves looking at the big-picture view, articulat-

ing broad project goals, and taking an honest look at options. This last step enables the organization to determine the best way to use internal resources and make the most of external resources.

7. Of the following, who developed a decision-making model for comparing potential vendors by dividing criteria into musts and wants and applying weightings to those items?

A. Kepner-Tregoe

Response A is correct because Charles H. Kepner and Benjamin B. Tregoe identified a practical, straightforward decision-making process that splits criteria into wants and musts and then weights those items.

8. Which of the following best describes a firm fixed-price contract?

A. The product or service can be clearly defined (for example, a presentation, video, or generic program).

Response A is correct because a firm fixed-price contract is used when a product or service has a fixed cost and a clear definition; this is much like purchasing a software program directly off a store shelf.

9. All the following are standard elements of an RFP *except*

D. Financial statements

Response D is correct because financial statements are not typically included in RFPs.

10. Which of the following is *not* a main step in the outsourcing process?

D. Conducting trainer interviews

Response D is correct because the steps in the outsourcing process are determining needs, defining the scope and budget, creating and sending the RFP, evaluating proposals and selecting a vendor, notifying the vendor and negotiating the contract, implementing the project, monitoring the schedule, and completing and evaluating the project. Interviewing trainers is not part of the vendor evaluation process.

11. Which of the following types of contracts requires analysis and development and also has a negotiated percentage of the overall cost identified as profit?

B. Cost plus fixed price

Response B is correct because a cost plus fixed price contract is often used by government procurement offices. With this type of contract, the vendor needs to do some analysis and development, but the total percentage of the vendor's profit is determined by the contract.

Chapter 7

1. A training director is developing a job description for a program administrator. Which of the following tasks best represents a program administrator's role?

D. Managing program elements to support training delivery

Response D is correct because administrating the program involves ensuring that the logistics are in place to ensure that the program takes place; in other words, the program administrator secures equipment and resources; identifies and trains instructors; manages course registration, scheduling, and locations; and works with SMEs as needed.

2. A manager of the learning function has been informed that budget cuts of 50 percent are being instituted across the organization. What programs should be cut?

D. The programs that aren't strategically aligned with the organization's goals and vision

Response D is correct because for the learning function to both be and appear valuable to the organization, and therefore not a function that can be cut, the WLP professional needs to ensure that programs that support the organization's goals remain in place, while those that aren't directly tied to those goals are cut.

3. A training manager is working on assigning trainers to courses for the next quarter. When making these staffing assignments, the primary considerations include all the following *except*

B. Trainer's ability to adhere firmly to the course outline

Response B is correct because the ability to adhere firmly to a course outline is not an important quality in a trainer; a trainer needs to be flexible to fulfill the specific needs of the learners.

4. A training manager's responsibilities include all the following *except*

D. Developing multimedia content to include in instruction

Response D is correct because it is not one of the training manager's responsibilities. That is part of the role of the training designer.

5. The learning objectives of instruction affect planning and selecting a facility.

A. True

Response A is correct because presentation techniques must be adapted to the ways that adults learn and because learning objectives dictate the best type of space to achieve the objectives. Therefore, a training manager must be mindful of the learning objectives before planning and selecting a facility.

6. A training director is developing a big-picture perspective of the types of courses and content the organization offers. What is this director developing?

C. Program curriculum

Response C is correct because a program curriculum encompasses all of the types of training that an organization offers.

7. Which of the following should *not* be a consideration when selecting an instructor?

A. Knowledge of the LMS and how to navigate

Response A is correct because the instructor has no need to understand the organization's LMS and how to navigate it. An LMS is used to manage the administrative functions of learning and is therefore not something the instructor, who is there to facilitate learning, really needs to know anything about.

8. SMEs are usually a project's primary content resource and have deep knowledge of designing and writing training materials.

B. False

Response B is correct because SMEs typically don't have deep knowledge of designing and writing training materials. They are, however, frequently the primary content resource.

9. When selecting an SME to help develop training, which of the following is an essential prerequisite?

B. Enthusiastic about his or her job

Response B is correct because enthusiasm about helping others to learn aids learning transfer. SMEs who don't want to impart their knowledge to others make bad trainers.

Chapter 8

1. Which of the following is *not* one of the four phases of strategic plan development?

A. Initiation

Response A is correct because initiation is not one of the phases of strategic plan development. The four phases are formulation, development, implementation, and evaluation.

2. In which phase of creating a strategic plan should a WLP professional conduct a SWOT analysis?

B. Development

Response B is correct because the first task in the development phase is to gather data, and this is done through a SWOT analysis, which gathers information about the department's strengths, weaknesses, opportunities, and threats. This information forms the basis upon which to develop the plan.

3. How often should strategic planning occur?

D. Continually and on an as-needed basis

Response D is correct because the purpose of a strategic plan is to enable training managers to accomplish more things that are critical to the training function and to the overall business strategy. For that reason, training managers need to continually revisit the strategic planning process as business needs evolve.

4. Objectives are designed to help WLP professionals identify how to carry out which of the following?

C. Strategic goals

Response C is correct because objectives are the component parts of strategic goals and specify tasks that will help to achieve the objectives.

5. During which of the following phases of strategic plan development does feedback and corrective action take place?

D. Evaluation

Response D is correct because the evaluation phase is where a feedback system is set up to provide information about the strategic plan's results.

6. A training department with a large in-house staff and numerous vendor partners is in the process of developing a strategic plan. Given the size of the training department, what is the likely role of the training manager in the strategic planning process?

D. Overseeing and focusing on future strategies for training

Response D is correct because in a large training department, in-house staff and vendors help meet the organization's needs, leaving the training manager to focus on the future vision and the strategies that will help the training function to reach that vision.

7. Which of the following best describes a chart of accounts?

A. A listing of account lines in the general ledger

Response A is correct because a chart of accounts is a list of all accounts tracked by an accounting system; each account in the list has a unique identifier known as an account number.

8. Which of the following best describes an economic resource that may be expressed in monetary terms?

A. Asset

Response A is correct because an asset is an economic resource that gives rise to future economic benefit and can be expressed in monetary terms.

9. Which of the following is *not* a source of prework research when forecasting a budget?

B. Participant demographics

Response B is correct because participant demographics do not provide the basis for forecasting a budget. Sources of prework research for a budget include the training plan, historical records of previous years' budgets, baseline funds, budget accuracy, benchmark data, and postmortems.

10. Which of the following is a comparison that weighs the cost of a training activity against the outcomes achieved?

A. Cost-benefit analysis

Response A is correct because a cost-benefit analysis compares the costs of training against the benefits gained from it to identify whether the investment in training paid off.

11. An example of a budget expense includes all the following *except*

D. Owner equity

Response D is correct because owner equity refers to the value of the owners' or shareholders' portion of the business after all claims against it have been subtracted and is not an expense item that would appear in a budget.

Chapter 9

1. An organization recently went through a restructuring and several rounds of downsizing employees. Despite budget cuts, the training manager is still expected to deliver training to meet the current client base. Which of the following activities should take top priority in this situation?

B. Motivating, inspiring, and aligning people with departmental and business goals

Response B is correct because ensuring that the training department's activities support the organization's goals by motivating, inspiring, and aligning the department's people to achieve those goals is the most productive way the training manager can achieve expectations.

2. A training manager is upset with the performance review he just received from his director. The manager cannot understand what the problem is. He regularly works long hours six days a week doing everything from instructional design to setting up the training rooms. The director indicated the poor review was a result of numerous complaints from the manager's direct reports. Which of the following tasks is the manager likely not adequately focusing on?

C. Providing vision, direction, values, and purpose to employees

Response C is correct because providing employees with vision, direction, values, and purpose is the part of a training manager's job that enables employees to understand what they are doing and why. Without this understanding, employees feel lost and feel as though their work is not appreciated.

3. To be a successful training manager, which of the following activities is most important?

B. Aligning people with departmental and business goals

Response B is correct because the role of the training manager is to enable the department to provide training that supports and furthers the organization's business goals. To do this, the training manager needs to ensure that his or her people work toward the goals of the department and of the business.

4. Which leadership function is concerned with setting goals and objectives, developing strategies, and establishing priorities?

B. Planning

Response B is correct because planning involves establishing objectives and setting a course or direction for achieving them.

5. Which leadership function is best described as ensuring that everything is performed and carried out according to plan?

D. Controlling

Response D is correct because controlling involves evaluating or assessing situations to ensure that everything happens according to plan.

6. A manager has received feedback that she needs to improve her planning skills. Which of the following activities should she focus on to better demonstrate her planning ability?

D. Establishing objectives and a direction to achieve them

Response D is correct because planning involves being able to set goals and objectives; develop strategies; establish priorities; and create timelines, work sequences, and budgets. Establishing objectives and a direction to achieve them is one way to demonstrate good planning abilities.

Chapter 10

1. A fundamental technique of project management is planning projects in phases. All of the phases that represent the project from beginning to end are collectively called

C. Life cycle

Response C is correct because the project life cycle includes everything that happens in a project from beginning to end.

2. Which of the following is *not* a standard phase name in the project life cycle?

A. Communicating

Response A is correct because communicating is not a standard phase name, although it is an important element in a successful project.

3. Which project phase is concerned with assigning resources to specific tasks and initiating the work?

B. Planning

Response B is correct because the planning phase is where the project manager and the team develop the project plan, the project manager plans the work and assigns resources to tasks, and the work is begun.

4. An example of a project management function is writing learning objectives.

B. False

Response B is correct because project management consists of planning, organizing, and controlling work. Even if writing learning objectives is part of the scope of the work, doing so is only a part of carrying out the project, not part of managing the project.

5. Which of the following involves ensuring that all of the project work—and only the approved project work—is completed?

A. Scope

Response A is correct because the project scope encompasses the work that was approved while defining the goals and objectives of the project. Controlling the project scope so that additional work that wasn't part of the original, approved plan—also known as scope creep—is an important part of the project manager's role.

6. Which of the following project team stakeholders and roles is defined as the person who controls the money and whose signature is needed to authorize purchases over a certain amount?

C. Budget client

Response C is correct because the budget client is the person who is accountable for the project's costs and how it will provide a return for the business.

As such, he or she pays for the project and has the power to cancel the project at any time.

7. Project time management includes processes required to ensure timely completion of the project. Which of the following is *not* a typical process used to support project time management?

A. Activity validation

Response A is correct because there is no process regarding validating the project's activities related to project time management.

8. Which project management tool is used in planning and integrating the project and represents a graphical hierarchy of the project, deliverables, tasks, and subtasks?

A. WBS

Response A is correct because the WBS is the primary tool to begin planning and documenting project deliverables. Project managers use it to identify tasks, subtasks, and units of work to be performed and create a hierarchy of those elements.

9. A project manager has been assigned to a new project and has finished collecting information. She is now developing several planning worksheets. Which of the following is she most likely creating?

D. Gantt chart

Response D is correct because Gantt charts are one of several planning worksheets that project managers use to plan the work of the project. Creating a Gantt chart involves creating a sequence of the tasks and subtasks of the work to create a milestone chart and mapping timeframe data onto it.

10. Which of the following represents the minimum time schedule for completing all tasks in a project and drives the project's end date?

C. Critical path

Response C is correct because the critical path represents the shortest period of time that it takes to complete all of the tasks in the project given task interdependencies.

11. A project manager is in the process of mapping the timeframe data for the project within a chart, which graphically displays the time relationships of the project's steps and deliverable dates. Which of the following is the project manager developing?

C. Gantt chart

Response C is correct because a Gantt chart maps tasks, subtasks, milestones, and timeframe data. Response A is incorrect because a WBS is a graphical representation of the hierarchy of the project's deliverables, tasks, and subtasks.

12. With the arrival of software tools such as automated Gantt charts and network-based analysis methods, the position of project manager is no longer necessary.

B. False

Response B is correct because these tools are simply management tools; they are not a substitute for project management. A major component of a project manager's job is to plan and control costs. A project's success depends largely on correctly estimating the level of effort and expenditures required.

13. Which of the following is best defined as work or deliverables that are added to a project but were not part of the initial approved plan nor added through a formal change?

D. Scope creep

Response D is correct because scope creep occurs when in the course of the project more work is added to the project that wasn't part of the original project scope.

Chapter 12

1. Reward management is primarily concerned with strategies using monetary compensation to drive employee performance.

B. False

Response B is correct because monetary compensation is not the only way to reward employees. Managers need to understand the seven basic needs of employees—achievement, power, affiliation, autonomy, esteem, safety and security, and equity—recognize the primary need motivating each person, and try to meet those needs through a variety of activities, only one of which is providing cash bonuses.

2. Performance management is primarily concerned with which of the following processes?

A. Developing, motivating, deploying, and aligning people to increase performance

Response A is correct because performance management involves enabling employees to meet business goals by helping them to learn needed skills, motivating them appropriately, and measuring their achievement against desired outcomes and metrics.

3. Which of the following is a computer-based system that HR professionals use to understand which employees need to develop required skills and experience?

A. Performance management

Response A is correct because a performance management system is used to determine what skills and knowledge employees need to work toward organizational goals.

4. The HR department of an organization is designing several new jobs. One of the goals of the design team is to develop jobs that employees will find interesting and motivating. Altering which of the following job factors is *least* likely to affect employee motivation?

B. Compensation

Response B is correct because compensation is not related to job design.

5. Training managers are responsible for helping the HR department plan short- and long-term goals based on changes occurring inside and outside the organization.

A. True

Response A is correct because organizations face constant change, and learning is one of the few features that enable organizations to adapt to change. To support the organization's long- and short-term business goals, the training function should consider its programs and policies and work closely with the HR department to enable it to be responsive to change.

6. Within the organization, training managers can use several strategies and tools to help motivate employees and drive desired behaviors. Which of the following is *not* one of those strategies or tools?

B. Realigning the organization, departments, and job roles frequently

Response B is correct because realigning the organization, departments, and job roles frequently can cause more harm than good in motivating

employees and driving desired behaviors. Frequent and unnecessary change can cause employees to become disoriented and feel insecure, thereby reducing their motivation.

7. It is the responsibility of the training function, not necessarily the HR department, to forecast future training needs.

B. False

Response B is correct because it is the responsibility of the HR department to examine corporate strategy roadmaps and marshal skills and resources the department may need to deliver training that will enable the organization to achieve its goals and objectives.

8. Compensation and reward systems are the best way to retain the best employees.

B. False

Response B is correct because employees who receive employee-sponsored training are more satisfied with their jobs and are more likely to stay with their employer than those who don't.

9. Conducting periodic job responsibility and KSA evaluations helps to accomplish which of the following objectives?

D. All of the above

Response D is correct because conducting periodic job responsibility and KSA evaluations helps to motivate employees, drive desired behaviors, and link individual goals with organizational goals.

Chapter 13

1. Organizational structures help to define department functions, roles and responsibilities, relationships among departments, reporting structures, and the flow of information.

A. True

Response A is correct because the ways that organizations are structured influences all of the ways that departments and individuals interact.

2. A business model is defined as a mechanism by which a business intends to generate revenue and profits and involves both the strategy and the implementation for defining product offerings, acquiring and keeping customers, the marketing strategy, and how it configures revenue and generates profit.

A. True

Response A is correct because a business model, which is also called a business design, summarizes how the company plans to serve its customers and involves strategy and implementation, as well as how the business selects customers, defines and differentiates product offerings, creates utility for customers, acquires and keeps customers, goes to the market, defines the tasks to be performed, configures resources, and captures profit.

3. Strategic business drivers are defined as

D. Internal and external forces that affect an organization's strategy, goals, business needs, and performance needs

Response D is correct because strategic business drivers are factors that affect how the organization does business. An example of an external business driver is government regulations, while an example of internal business driver is technology.

4. An organization's culture is defined as the assumptions employees share about their work and feelings toward the organization.

A. True

Response A is correct because organizational culture refers to the shared values within the organization that govern the nature of organizational relationships, the types of people hired, performance and promotion criteria, rewards and censure, work climate, and management style.

5. A training director new to the company spends much of his first few weeks learning about the company's history, mission, goals, strategy, tactics, vision, and plans. This information will help the new director understand which of the following?

A. Company's culture

Response A is correct because the company's culture encompasses all of the ways that things are done in an organization. Therefore, understanding the company's history, mission, goals, strategy, tactics, vision, and plans are good places to learn about how things get done in the organization.

6. Assessing an organization's culture is *not* required for successfully implementing most small initiatives.

B. False

Response B is correct because understanding how the organization's culture will help or hinder change is critical.

7. Which of the following environmental factors includes technology, new products, and changes in systems processes or policies?

D. Internal

Response D is correct because internal factors encompass forces within the organization that can affect its strategy and goals. Examples include changes in systems, processes, or policies that may require changes in employee skills and behavior.

8. Which of the following environmental factors includes economic changes, HR, and skill shortages?

B. External

Response B is correct because external factors encompass forces from outside the organization that affect the organization's strategy and goals and include economic changes, HR and skill shortages, governmental decisions, public perception, and market or customer requirements.

9. A director of a training department is criticized by company leadership for "signing off" on poor training vendor agreements. Which of the following environmental factors is this director not adequately managing?

A. Contractual

Response A is correct because contractual factors include stipulations laid out in vendor agreements for services and raw materials.

10. A small consulting firm has more work than it can deliver. Although the firm has tried to hire additional consultants, no qualified candidates can be located. Which of the following environmental factors is negatively affecting this company?

C. Employees

Response C is correct because employee factors include shortages in the number of employees or in the number of employees with a certain skill set.

Chapter 14

1. New legislation and a partisan climate are examples of which of the following external

environmental factors that may influence an organization?

B. Political

Response B is correct because political factors include level of privatization in government services, political trends affecting suppliers and customers, and level of partisanship in governmental bodies.

2. Which of the following analyses can help WLP professionals scan the environment and analyze current and future trends and forces?

A. SWOT

Response A is correct because a WLP professional can use an environmental scan and a SWOT (strengths, weaknesses, opportunities, and threats) analysis to take an inventory of external factors and trends and to gain insight into the corporate plan.

3. A geopolitical scan is an inventory of the political, economic, sociological, cultural, global, technological, and employment forces that influence the way an organization functions.

B. False

Response B is correct because an inventory of political, economic, sociological, cultural, global, technological, and employment forces is called an environmental scan.

4. Worker skills, corporate responsibilities and ethics, population shifts, immigration, migration, age, and gender are examples of which of the following external environmental factors that may influence an organization?

C. Sociological

Response C is correct because sociological factors encompass broad forces that affect a population, including generational differences, minority groups, and nontraditional labor.

5. As a result of the last U.S. presidential election, a training director is anticipating the need to increase the amount of OSHA compliance training. Which external environmental factor is this director adjusting to?

B. Political

Response B is correct because, in the example, political changes have affected the level of compli-

ance training required of the organization. This is an example of a political factor that has influenced the way that the organization does its business.

6. With the advent of automated project management software, clients are starting to expect weekly PERT and Gantt chart updates. Because of these new expectations, a consulting firm needed to change its project management process. Which external environmental factor is this company adjusting to?

B. Technological

Response B is correct because the example illustrates a change in technology, in this case the more frequent use of project management software, changing the way an organization carries out its business.

7. Which of the following is an example of an external relationship that affects an organization?

A. Customers

Response A is correct because customers are one type of external relationship that affects how an organization does business. Others include vendors, competitors, community, charities, and employees.

Chapter 15

1. According to EEOC laws, HR professionals and training managers need to be careful about the selection of someone for a training program because these criteria and selection process are considered a test.

A. True

Response A is correct because a decision to select someone for a training program is considered a test. For example, an interview to determine eligibility for a training opportunity is just as much a test under the law as a requirement to pass pencil-and-paper assessment of verbal fluency for entry into an organizationally sponsored program.

2. Important legal issues for HR and the training function involving lawful selection of people to participate in WLP programs include all the following *except*

D. Assigning job based on performance in previous job roles

Response D is correct because performance in previous job roles is an appropriate and nondiscriminatory criterion that can be used to determine if a person can participate in a WLP program. Performance in previous job roles is an example of a criterion that is job related.

3. An outdoor experiential team-building training program that a vendor offers includes rigorous adventure activities, such as whitewater rafting. One employee refuses to attend because the program takes place on a Saturday, which she observes as a religious holiday. If the organization insists that she attend or face termination, which of the following laws is in violation?

C. Civil rights

Response C is correct because civil rights law guarantees against discrimination in employment based on certain civil rights, including the right to privacy and the right of equal protection.

4. Which of the following is *not* an example of a reasonable accommodation that the training function must provide for people with disabilities?

C. Customized one-on-one training

Response C is correct because providing customized one-on-one training is an unreasonable accommodation for a disabled person.

5. An instructional designer needs to include information on current legislation regarding fork lift safety in her training class. Which of the following is the official source charged with providing specific safety standards?

B. Secretary of Labor

Response B is correct because the U.S. Congress determined that the Secretary of Labor promulgates specific safety standards for each industry under OSHA.

6. The Sarbanes-Oxley Act of 2002 affects which of the following types of legislation?

D. Security and financial reporting

Response D is correct because the Sarbanes-Oxley Act was passed to protect investors from fraudulent accounting activities by improving the accuracy and reliability of corporate financial disclosures.

7. To comply with national IT standards, IT training managers must provide access to courses and programs for the IT group.

A. True

Response A is correct because national IT standards were established to ensure that all IT systems and architecture work together. To ensure that the IT departments comply with these standards and to help IT departments stay ahead of the IT curve and use new technologies in the organization, training managers must provide access to training.

8. A training department is responsible for training a large number of unionized employees. How will unions most likely affect the training provided to employees?

C. Unions help define the skill levels associated with job titles.

Response C is correct because labor reforms of the 1930s reorganized many unions on an industry-wide basis, mixing skills and unskilled workers in the same union. Distinctions regarding mastery of skills were dealt with through contract language, thereby leaving unions with a leading role in defining skill levels associated with job titles or craft titles.

9. Which of the following is *not* one of the exclusive rights of copyright holders?

C. To copyright the initial idea that the copyrighted work was derived from

Response C is correct because copyright protection does not cover ideas, concepts, or facts; copyright covers the expression of ideas, concepts, and facts. Therefore, it is not possible to copyright the idea upon which the work was based.

10. A WLP professional needs to distribute copies but is not sure the fair use doctrine applies. Then, the WLP professional notices that the copyright date is five years old; therefore, the copyright privileges no longer apply to the published information.

B. False

Response B is correct because it is inaccurate to assume that copyright privilege ceases to protect a copyrighted work after only five years. The period of protection lasts for 75 years from the date of first publication or 100 years after the year of creation, whatever expires first.

11. Which of the following is *not* an example of corporate policy and procedure documentation?

C. Intellectual property laws

Response C is correct because intellectual property laws are not an example of corporate policy and procedure documentation. Intellectual property laws encompass a body of law related to copyright protection, patent law, and so forth.

12. Ethical standards for WLP professionals include professional association guidelines; industry standards; codes of conduct; and self-governing behaviors, including honesty, integrity, respect, and accountability.

A. True

Response A is correct because ethics encompass a set of moral principles, rules, and standards of conduct. Some of these rules are found in industry codes of behavior, such as professional association guidelines, industry standards, and codes of conduct. Others are more personal in nature, such as self-governing behaviors, that arise from an individual's sense of morality.

Appendix C
Index

Note: *f* represents a figure and *t* represents a table.

**ASTD Learning System
Editorial Staff**

Director: Anthony Allen
Manager: Larry Fox
Editors: Tora Estep, Ashley McDonald
Editorial Assistant: Stephanie Castellano

Contributing Editors

April Michelle Davis, Stephanie Sussan

Proofreader

Kris Patenaude

Graphic Designer

Kathleen Schaner

Indexer

April Michelle Davis

Thomson NETg Staff

Solutions Manager: Robyn Rickenbach
Director: John Pydyn

Contributing Writers

Lynn Lewis, Dawn Rader

Editors

Lisa Lord, Kim Lindros, Karen Day

Thomson NETg, formerly backed
by the Thomson Corporation, was a
global enterprise comprised of a vast
array of world-renowned publishing
and information assets in the areas of
academics, business and government,
financial services, science and healthcare, and the law. NETg was acquired
by SkillSoft in 2007.

ASTD (American Society for Training
& Development) is the world's largest
association dedicated to workplace
learning and performance professionals.
ASTD's 70,000 members and associates
come from more than 100 countries
and thousands of organizations—
multinational corporations, medium-
sized and small businesses, government,
academia, consulting firms, and product
and service suppliers.

ASTD marks its beginning in 1944 when
the organization held its first annual
conference. In recent years, ASTD has
widened the industry's focus to connect
learning and performance to measurable
results and is a sought-after voice on
critical public policy issues.